www.EffortlessMath.com

... So Much More Online!

✓ FREE Math lessons

✓ More Math learning books!

✓ Mathematics Worksheets

✓ Online Math Tutors

Need a PDF version of this book?

Visit www.EffortlessMath.com

5 Full-Length SSAT Upper Level Math Practice Tests

The Practice You Need to Ace the SSAT Upper Level Math Test

By

Reza Nazari

& Ava Ross

All inquiries should be addressed to:

info@effortlessMath.com

www.EffortlessMath.com

ISBN–13: 978-1-64612-106-9

ISBN–10: 1-64612-106-6

Published by: Effortless Math Education

www.EffortlessMath.com

Description

5 Full-Length SSAT Upper Level Math Practice Tests, which reflects the 2020 and 2021 test guidelines and topics, is designed to help you hone your math skills, overcome your exam anxiety, and boost your confidence -- and do your best to ace the SSAT Upper Level Math Test. The realistic and full-length SSAT Upper Level Math tests show you how the test is structured and what math topics you need to master. The practice test questions are followed by answer explanations to help you find your weak areas, learn from your mistakes, and raise your SSAT Upper Level Math score.

The surest way to succeed on SSAT Upper Level Math Test is with intensive practice in every math topic tested-- and that's what you will get in ***5 Full-Length SSAT Upper Level Math Practice Tests***. This SSAT Upper Level Math new edition has been updated to replicate questions appearing on the most recent SSAT Upper Level Math tests. This is a precious learning tool for SSAT Upper Level Math test takers who need extra practice in math to improve their SSAT Math score. After taking the SSAT Math practice tests in this book, you will have solid foundation and adequate practice that is necessary to succeed on the SSAT Upper Level Math test. **This book is your ticket to ace the SSAT Upper Level Math!**

5 Full-Length SSAT Upper Level Math Practice Tests contains many exciting and unique features to help you improve your test scores, including:

- Content 100% aligned with the 2020 – 2021 SSAT Upper Level test
- Written by SSAT Math tutors and test experts
- Complete coverage of all SSAT Upper Level Math concepts and topics which you will be tested
- Detailed answers and explanations for every SSAT Upper Level Math practice questions to help you learn from your mistakes
- 5 full-length practice tests (featuring new question types) with detailed answers

This SSAT Upper Level Math book and other Effortless Math Education books are used by thousands of students each year to help them review core content areas, brush-up in math, discover their strengths and weaknesses, and achieve their best scores on the SSAT Upper Level test.

About the Author

Reza Nazari is the author of more than 100 Math learning books including:
– **Math and Critical Thinking Challenges:** For the Middle and High School Student
– **GRE Math in 30 Days**
– **ASVAB Math Workbook**
– **Effortless Math Education Workbooks**
– **and many more Mathematics books ...**

Reza is also an experienced Math instructor and a test–prep expert who has been tutoring students since 2008. Reza is the founder of Effortless Math Education, a tutoring company that has helped many students raise their standardized test scores—and attend the colleges of their dreams. Reza provides an individualized custom learning plan and the personalized attention that makes a difference in how students view math.

You can contact Reza via email at:
reza@EffortlessMath.com

Find Reza's professional profile at:
goo.gl/zoC9rJ

SSAT Upper Level Test Review

The SSAT, or Secondary School Admissions Test, is a standardized test to help determine admission to private elementary, middle and high schools.

There are currently three Levels of the SSAT:

- ✓ Lower Level (for students in 3rd and 4th grade)
- ✓ Middle Level (for students in 5th-7th grade)
- ✓ Upper Level (for students in 8th-11th grade)

There are six sections on the SSAT Upper Level Test:

- ✓ Writing: 25 minutes.
- ✓ Math section: 25 questions, 30 minutes
- ✓ Reading section: 40 questions, 40 minutes
- ✓ Verbal section: 60 questions, 30 minutes
- ✓ Math section: 25 questions, 30 minutes
- ✓ Experimental: 16 questions, 15 minutes.

In this book, there are 5 complete SSAT Upper Level Math Practice Tests. Take these tests to see what score you'll be able to receive on a real SSAT Upper Level test.

Good luck!

Time to Test

Time to refine your skill with a practice examination

Take a practice SSAT Upper Level Mathematics Test to simulate the test day experience. After you've finished, score your test using the answer keys.

Before You Start

- You'll need a pencil and a timer to take the test.
- Each test contains 25 multiple-choice questions. For each question, there are five possible answers. Choose which one is best.
- After you've finished the test, review the answer key to see where you went wrong.
- Use the answer sheet provided to record your answers. (You can cut it out or photocopy it)
- You will receive 1 point for every correct answer, and you will lose $\frac{1}{4}$ point for each incorrect answer. There is no penalty for skipping a question.

Calculators are NOT permitted for the SSAT Upper Level Test

Good Luck!

SSAT Upper Level Math Practice Test 1

2020 - 2021

Two Parts

Total number of questions: 50

Section 1: 25 questions

Section 2: 25 questions

Total time for two parts: 60 Minutes

SSAT Upper Level Math Practice Test 1 Answer Sheet

Remove (or photocopy) this answer sheet and use it to complete the practice test.

SSAT Upper Level Mathematics Practice Test 1 Answer Sheet

SSAT Upper Level Practice Section 1

1	Ⓐ Ⓑ Ⓒ Ⓓ Ⓔ	11	Ⓐ Ⓑ Ⓒ Ⓓ Ⓔ	21	Ⓐ Ⓑ Ⓒ Ⓓ Ⓔ
2	Ⓐ Ⓑ Ⓒ Ⓓ Ⓔ	12	Ⓐ Ⓑ Ⓒ Ⓓ Ⓔ	22	Ⓐ Ⓑ Ⓒ Ⓓ Ⓔ
3	Ⓐ Ⓑ Ⓒ Ⓓ Ⓔ	13	Ⓐ Ⓑ Ⓒ Ⓓ Ⓔ	23	Ⓐ Ⓑ Ⓒ Ⓓ Ⓔ
4	Ⓐ Ⓑ Ⓒ Ⓓ Ⓔ	14	Ⓐ Ⓑ Ⓒ Ⓓ Ⓔ	24	Ⓐ Ⓑ Ⓒ Ⓓ Ⓔ
5	Ⓐ Ⓑ Ⓒ Ⓓ Ⓔ	15	Ⓐ Ⓑ Ⓒ Ⓓ Ⓔ	25	Ⓐ Ⓑ Ⓒ Ⓓ Ⓔ
6	Ⓐ Ⓑ Ⓒ Ⓓ Ⓔ	16	Ⓐ Ⓑ Ⓒ Ⓓ Ⓔ		
7	Ⓐ Ⓑ Ⓒ Ⓓ Ⓔ	17	Ⓐ Ⓑ Ⓒ Ⓓ Ⓔ		
8	Ⓐ Ⓑ Ⓒ Ⓓ Ⓔ	18	Ⓐ Ⓑ Ⓒ Ⓓ Ⓔ		
9	Ⓐ Ⓑ Ⓒ Ⓓ Ⓔ	19	Ⓐ Ⓑ Ⓒ Ⓓ Ⓔ		
10	Ⓐ Ⓑ Ⓒ Ⓓ Ⓔ	20	Ⓐ Ⓑ Ⓒ Ⓓ Ⓔ		

SSAT Upper Level Practice Section 2

1	Ⓐ Ⓑ Ⓒ Ⓓ Ⓔ	11	Ⓐ Ⓑ Ⓒ Ⓓ Ⓔ	21	Ⓐ Ⓑ Ⓒ Ⓓ Ⓔ
2	Ⓐ Ⓑ Ⓒ Ⓓ Ⓔ	12	Ⓐ Ⓑ Ⓒ Ⓓ Ⓔ	22	Ⓐ Ⓑ Ⓒ Ⓓ Ⓔ
3	Ⓐ Ⓑ Ⓒ Ⓓ Ⓔ	13	Ⓐ Ⓑ Ⓒ Ⓓ Ⓔ	23	Ⓐ Ⓑ Ⓒ Ⓓ Ⓔ
4	Ⓐ Ⓑ Ⓒ Ⓓ Ⓔ	14	Ⓐ Ⓑ Ⓒ Ⓓ Ⓔ	24	Ⓐ Ⓑ Ⓒ Ⓓ Ⓔ
5	Ⓐ Ⓑ Ⓒ Ⓓ Ⓔ	15	Ⓐ Ⓑ Ⓒ Ⓓ Ⓔ	25	Ⓐ Ⓑ Ⓒ Ⓓ Ⓔ
6	Ⓐ Ⓑ Ⓒ Ⓓ Ⓔ	16	Ⓐ Ⓑ Ⓒ Ⓓ Ⓔ		
7	Ⓐ Ⓑ Ⓒ Ⓓ Ⓔ	17	Ⓐ Ⓑ Ⓒ Ⓓ Ⓔ		
8	Ⓐ Ⓑ Ⓒ Ⓓ Ⓔ	18	Ⓐ Ⓑ Ⓒ Ⓓ Ⓔ		
9	Ⓐ Ⓑ Ⓒ Ⓓ Ⓔ	19	Ⓐ Ⓑ Ⓒ Ⓓ Ⓔ		
10	Ⓐ Ⓑ Ⓒ Ⓓ Ⓔ	20	Ⓐ Ⓑ Ⓒ Ⓓ Ⓔ		

SSAT Upper Level Math

Practice Test 1

Section 1

25 questions

Total time for this section: 30 Minutes

You may NOT use a calculator for this test.

1) A school wants to give each of its 22 top students a football ball. If the balls are in boxes of four, how many boxes of balls they need to purchase?
   A. 2
   B. 4
   C. 6
   D. 8
   E. 22

2) A shaft rotates 240 times in 12 seconds. How many times does it rotate in 20 seconds?
   A. 450
   B. 400
   C. 300
   D. 250
   E. 200

3) What is the value of x in the following figure?
   A. 150
   B. 145
   C. 135
   D. 125
   E. 115

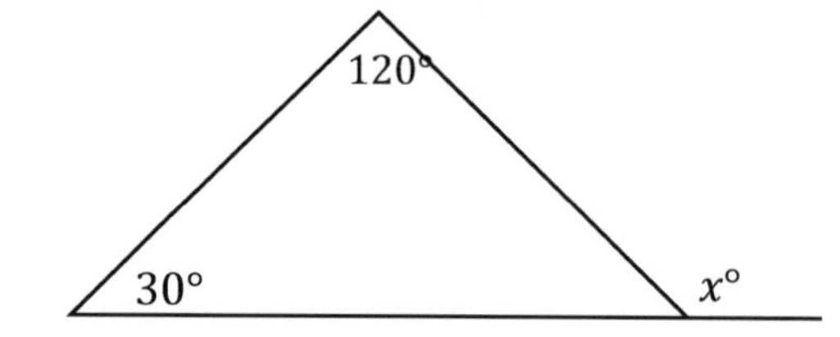

4) $14.125 \div 0.005$?
   A. 2.825
   B. 28.250
   C. 282.50
   D. 2825
   E. 28025

5) How many tiles of $5\ cm^2$ is needed to cover a floor of dimension $5\ cm$ by $20\ cm$?
   A. 5
   B. 10
   C. 15
   D. 20
   E. 25

6) If $\frac{30}{A} + 1 = 7$, then $30 + A = ?$
   A. 2
   B. 7
   C. 35
   D. 40
   E. 50

7) What is the value of the sum of the tens and thousandths in number 3,617.89652?
   A. 16
   B. 11
   C. 8
   D. 7
   E. 4

8) Jack earns $720 for his first 45 hours of work in a week and is then paid 1.5 times his regular hourly rate for any additional hours. This week, Jack needs $936 to pay his rent, bills and other expenses. How many hours must he work to make enough money in this week?
   A. 50
   B. 54
   C. 60
   D. 63
   E. 64

9) If 50% of a number is 85, then what is the 20% of that number?
   A. 34
   B. 40
   C. 50
   D. 60
   E. 85

10) Which of the following statements is correct, according to the graph below?

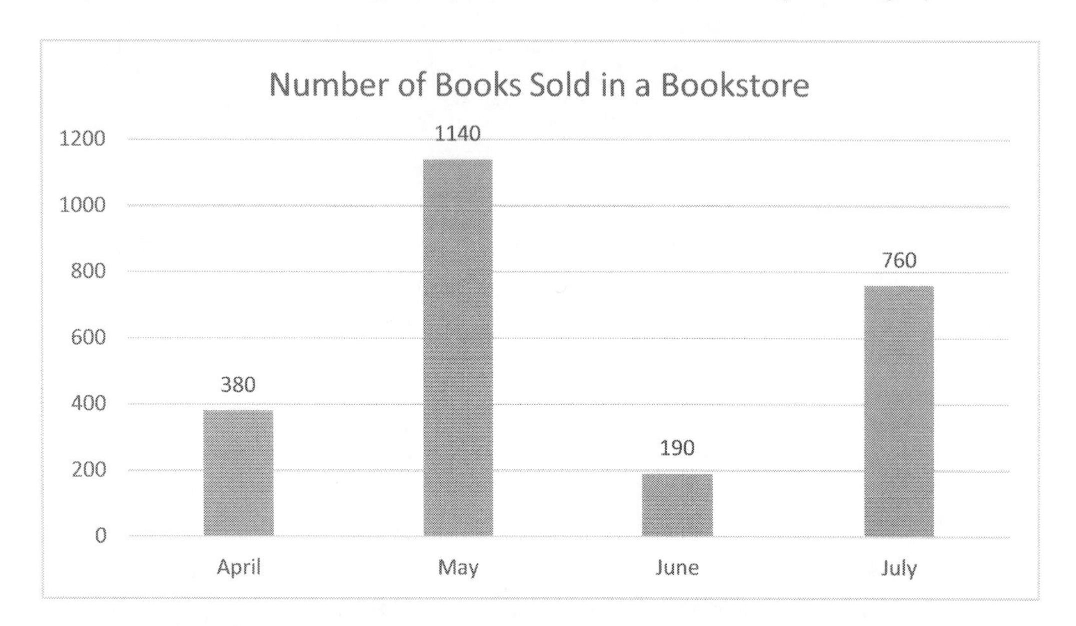

A. Number of books sold in April was twice the number of books sold in July.
B. Number of books sold in July was less than half the number of books sold in May.
C. Number of books sold in June was half the number of books sold in April.
D. Number of books sold in July was equal to the number of books sold in April plus the number of books sold in June.
E. More books were sold in April than in July.

11) If $x \blacksquare y = \sqrt{x^2 + y}$, what is the value of $6 \blacksquare 28$?
A. $\sqrt{168}$
B. 10
C. 8
D. 6
E. 4

12) If $2 \leq x < 6$, what is the minimum value of the following expression?

$$3x + 1$$

A. 9
B. 7
C. 4
D. 2
E. 1

13) What is the answer of $0.9 \div 0.015$?

A. $\frac{1}{60}$
B. $\frac{1}{6}$
C. 6
D. 60
E. 600

14) $\frac{1\frac{4}{3}+\frac{1}{4}}{2\frac{1}{2}-\frac{17}{8}}$ is approximately equal to.

A. 3.33
B. 3.6
C. 5.67
D. 6.88
E. 6.97

15) There are four equal tanks of water. If $\frac{2}{5}$ of a tank contains 300 liters of water, what is the capacity of the four tanks of water together?

A. $1{,}500$ liters
B. $2{,}000$ liters
C. $2{,}500$ liters
D. $3{,}000$ liters
E. $3{,}500$ liters

16) A cruise line ship left Port A and traveled 30 miles due west and then 40 miles due north. At this point, what is the shortest distance from the cruise to port A?

A. 50 miles
B. 55 miles
C. 60 miles
D. 70 miles
E. 110 miles

17) The average weight of 20 girls in a class is $55\ kg$ and the average weight of 42 boys in the same class is $82\ kg$. What is the average weight of all the 62 students in that class?

A. $70\ kg$
B. $72.20\ kg$
C. $73.29\ kg$
D. $74.44\ kg$
E. $75.20\ kg$

18) Two-kilograms apple and two-kilograms orange cost $\$28.4$. If one-kilogram apple costs $\$5.2$, how much does one-kilogram orange cost?
   A. $\$9$
   B. $\$6.5$
   C. $\$6$
   D. $\$5.5$
   E. $\$5$

19) David's current age is 44 years, and Ava's current age is 4 years old. In how many years David's age will be 5 times Ava's age?
   A. 4
   B. 6
   C. 8
   D. 10
   E. 14

20) Michelle and Alec can finish a job together in 50 minutes. If Michelle can do the job by herself in 2.5 hours, how many minutes does it take Alec to finish the job?
   A. 60
   B. 75
   C. 80
   D. 100
   E. 150

21) The sum of six different negative integers is -80. If the smallest of these integers is -16, what is the largest possible value of one of the other five integers?
   A. -16
   B. -10
   C. -8
   D. -4
   E. -1

22) What is the slope of a line that is perpendicular to the line $2x - 4y = 24$?
   A. -2
   B. $-\frac{1}{2}$
   C. 6
   D. 12
   E. 14

23) The width of a box is one third of its length. The height of the box is one half of its width. If the length of the box is $24\ cm$, what is the volume of the box?

A. $91\ cm^3$
B. $172\ cm^3$
C. $254\ cm^3$
D. $768\ cm^3$
E. $2{,}990\ cm^3$

24) A football team won exactly 70% of the games it played during last session. Which of the following could be the total number of games the team played last season?

A. 59
B. 45
C. 72
D. 20
E. 11

25) The Jackson Library is ordering some bookshelves. If x is the number of bookshelves the library wants to order, which each costs \$200 and there is a one-time delivery charge of \$600, which of the following represents the total cost, in dollar, per bookshelf?

A. $\frac{200x+600}{x}$
B. $\frac{200x+600}{200}$
C. $200 + 600x$
D. $200x + 600$
E. $200x - 600$

IF YOU FINISH BEFORE TIME IS CALLED, YOU MAY CHECK YOUR WORK ON THIS SECTION ONLY. DO NOT TURN TO ANY OTHER SECTION IN THE TEST.

STOP

SSAT Upper Level Math

Practice Test 1

Section 2

25 questions

Total time for this section: 30 Minutes

You may NOT use a calculator for this test.

1) There are 14 marbles in the bag A and 18 marbles in the bag B. If the sum of the marbles in both bags will be shared equally between two children, how many marbles bag A has less than the marbles that each child will receive?
   A. 2
   B. 3
   C. 4
   D. 5
   E. 6

2) If Jason's mark is F more than Alex, and Jason's mark is 18, which of the following can be Alex's mark?
   A. $18 - F$
   B. $F - 18$
   C. $\frac{F}{18}$
   D. $18F$
   E. $18 + F$

3) When number $81{,}602$ is divided by 240, the result is closest to?
   A. 4
   B. 30
   C. 200
   D. 300
   E. 340

4) The price of a sofa is decreased by 50% to $\$530$. What was its original price?
   A. $\$580$
   B. $\$620$
   C. $\$760$
   D. $\$900$
   E. $\$1{,}060$

5) If the perimeter of the following figure be 33, what is the value of x?
   A. 3
   B. 4
   C. 6
   D. 8
   E. 11

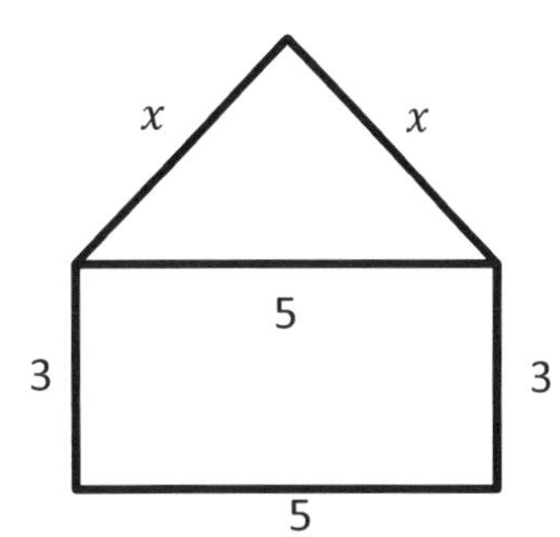

6) To paint a wall with the area of $57m^2$, how many liters of paint do we need if each liter of paint is enough to paint a wall with dimension of $80\ cm \times 95\ cm$?
   A. 50
   B. 75
   C. 100
   D. 150
   E. 200

7) Which of the following expression is not equal to 6?
   A. $12 \times \frac{1}{2}$
   B. $24 \times \frac{1}{4}$
   C. $2 \times \frac{6}{2}$
   D. $5 \times \frac{6}{5}$
   E. $6 \times \frac{1}{6}$

8) $760 - 9\frac{8}{14} = ?$
   A. $750\frac{3}{7}$
   B. $750\frac{8}{7}$
   C. $753\frac{1}{7}$
   D. $753\frac{8}{7}$
   E. $754\frac{1}{7}$

9) What is the missing term in the given sequence?

$$3, 4, 6, 9, 13, 18, 24, \_\_, 39$$

   A. 25
   B. 27
   C. 28
   D. 29
   E. 31

10) A driver rests one hour and 15 minutes for every 3 hours driving. How many minutes will he rest if he drives 24 hours?
   A. $3\ hours\ and\ 26\ minutest$
   B. $4\ hours\ and\ 10\ minutest$
   C. $5\ hours\ and\ 36\ minutest$
   D. $6\ hours\ and\ 46\ minutest$
   E. $10\ hours$

11) If $5y + 5 < 30$, then y could be equal to?

A. 14
B. 11
C. 9.5
D. 5
E. 3

12) If the area of the following rectangular $ABCD$ is 160, and E is the midpoint of AB, what is the area of the shaded part?

A. 30
B. 60
C. 70
D. 80
E. 90

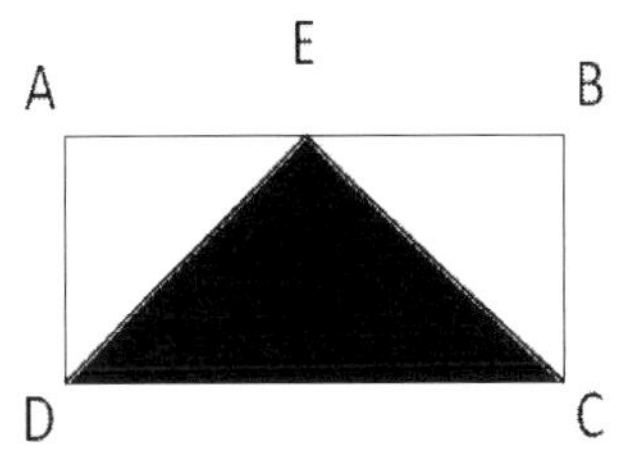

Questions 13 to 14 are based on the following graph

A library has 840 books that include Mathematics, Physics, Chemistry, English and History. Use following graph to answer questions 13 to 14.

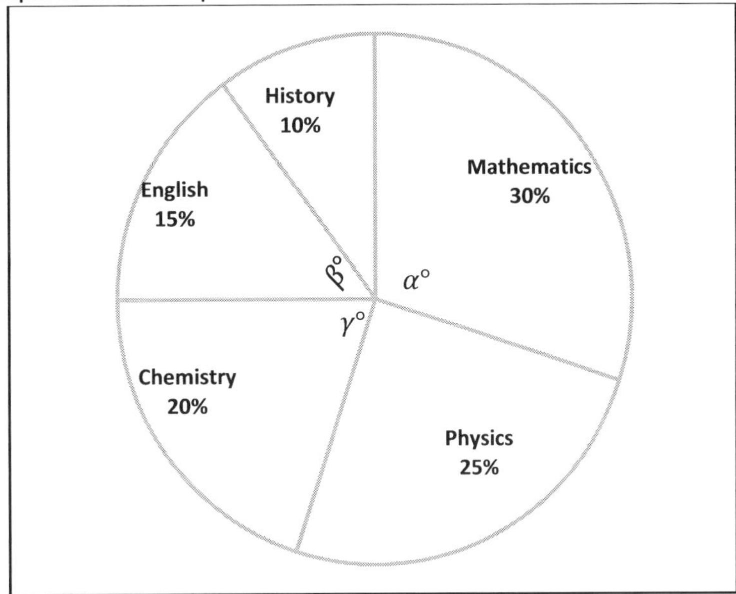

13) What is the product of the number of Mathematics and number of English books?

A. $21,168$
B. $31,752$
C. $26,460$
D. $17,640$
E. $35,280$

14) What are the values of angle α and β respectively?
A. $90°, 54°$
B. $120°, 36°$
C. $120°, 45°$
D. $108°, 54°$
E. $108°, 45°$

15) The capacity of a red box is 20% bigger than the capacity of a blue box. If the red box can hold 60 equal sized books, how many of the same books can the blue box hold?
A. 15
B. 25
C. 40
D. 50
E. 60

16) If $8x + y = 24$ and $x - z = 17$, what is the value of x?
A. 1
B. 4
C. 9
D. 19
E. it cannot be determined from the information given

17) Find the perimeter of following shape.

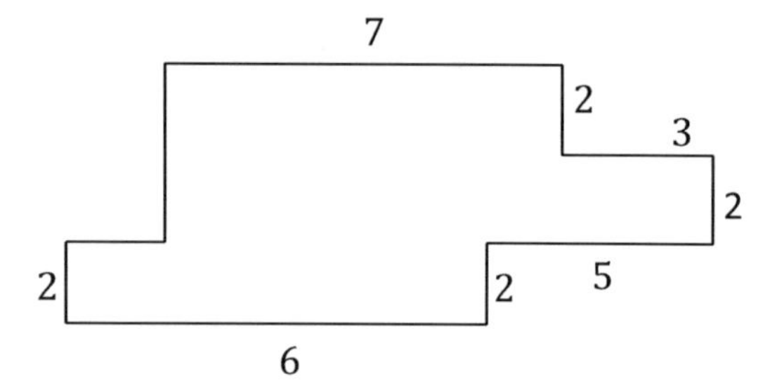

A. 20
B. 21
C. 22
D. 30
E. 34

18) There are 60.4 liters of gas in a car fuel tank. In the first week and second week of April, the car uses 4.86 and 23.9 liters of gas respectively. If the car was park in the third week of April and 11.22 liters of gas will be added to the fuel tank, how many liters of gas are in the fuel tank of the car?
A. 20.41 liters
B. 26.5 liters
C. 28 liters
D. 28.79 liters
E. 42.86 liters

19) If $a \times b$ is divisible by 4, which of the following expression must also be divisible by 4?

A. $2a - 5b$
B. $3a - b$
C. $2a \times 3b$
D. $\frac{a}{b}$
E. $\frac{a \times b}{3}$

20) Which of the following could be the value of x if $\frac{6}{8} + x > 2$?

A. $\frac{1}{3}$
B. $\frac{3}{5}$
C. $\frac{6}{5}$
D. $\frac{4}{3}$
E. $\frac{2}{3}$

21) If a gas tank can hold 20 gallons, how many gallons does it contain when it is $\frac{3}{4}$ full?

A. 135
B. 52.5
C. 50
D. 20
E. 15

22) In the following figure, point Q lies on line n, what is the value of y if $x = 35$?

A. 10
B. 25
C. 30
D. 40
E. 50

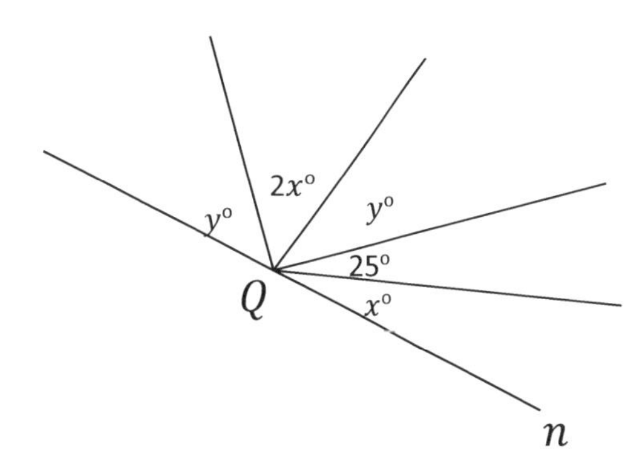

23) A number is chosen at random from 1 to 20. Find the probability of not selecting a composite number. (A composite number is a number that is divisible by itself, 1 and at least one other whole number)

A. $\frac{1}{20}$
B. $\frac{2}{5}$
C. $\frac{9}{20}$
D. 1
E. 0

24) $615 \div 4 = ?$

A. $\frac{600}{4} \times \frac{10}{4} \times \frac{5}{4}$
B. $600 + \frac{10}{4} + \frac{5}{4}$
C. $\frac{600}{4} + \frac{10}{4} + \frac{5}{4}$
D. $\frac{600}{4} \div \frac{10}{4} \div \frac{5}{4}$
E. $\frac{6}{4} + \frac{1}{4} + \frac{5}{4}$

25) What is the average of circumference of figure A and area of figure B? ($\pi = 3$)

A. 75
B. 70
C. 60
D. 50
E. 44

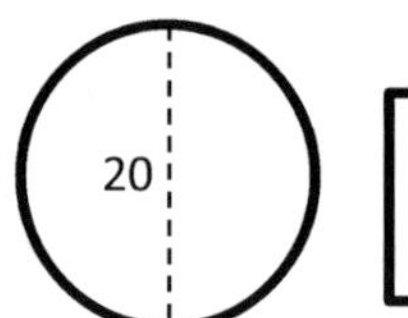

Figure A

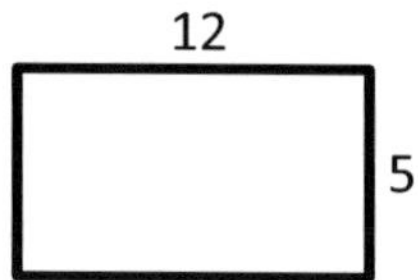

Figure B

IF YOU FINISH BEFORE TIME IS CALLED, YOU MAY CHECK YOUR WORK ON THIS SECTION ONLY. DO NOT TURN TO ANY OTHER SECTION IN THE TEST.

STOP

SSAT Upper Level Math Practice Test 2

2020 - 2021

Two Parts

Total number of questions: 50

Section 1: 25 questions

Section 2: 25 questions

Total time for two parts: 60 Minutes

SSAT Upper Level Math Practice Test 2 Answer Sheet

Remove (or photocopy) this answer sheet and use it to complete the practice test.

SSAT Upper Level Mathematics Practice Test 2 Answer Sheet

SSAT Upper Level Math Section 1

1	Ⓐ Ⓑ Ⓒ Ⓓ Ⓔ	11	Ⓐ Ⓑ Ⓒ Ⓓ Ⓔ	21	Ⓐ Ⓑ Ⓒ Ⓓ Ⓔ
2	Ⓐ Ⓑ Ⓒ Ⓓ Ⓔ	12	Ⓐ Ⓑ Ⓒ Ⓓ Ⓔ	22	Ⓐ Ⓑ Ⓒ Ⓓ Ⓔ
3	Ⓐ Ⓑ Ⓒ Ⓓ Ⓔ	13	Ⓐ Ⓑ Ⓒ Ⓓ Ⓔ	23	Ⓐ Ⓑ Ⓒ Ⓓ Ⓔ
4	Ⓐ Ⓑ Ⓒ Ⓓ Ⓔ	14	Ⓐ Ⓑ Ⓒ Ⓓ Ⓔ	24	Ⓐ Ⓑ Ⓒ Ⓓ Ⓔ
5	Ⓐ Ⓑ Ⓒ Ⓓ Ⓔ	15	Ⓐ Ⓑ Ⓒ Ⓓ Ⓔ	25	Ⓐ Ⓑ Ⓒ Ⓓ Ⓔ
6	Ⓐ Ⓑ Ⓒ Ⓓ Ⓔ	16	Ⓐ Ⓑ Ⓒ Ⓓ Ⓔ		
7	Ⓐ Ⓑ Ⓒ Ⓓ Ⓔ	17	Ⓐ Ⓑ Ⓒ Ⓓ Ⓔ		
8	Ⓐ Ⓑ Ⓒ Ⓓ Ⓔ	18	Ⓐ Ⓑ Ⓒ Ⓓ Ⓔ		
9	Ⓐ Ⓑ Ⓒ Ⓓ Ⓔ	19	Ⓐ Ⓑ Ⓒ Ⓓ Ⓔ		
10	Ⓐ Ⓑ Ⓒ Ⓓ Ⓔ	20	Ⓐ Ⓑ Ⓒ Ⓓ Ⓔ		

SSAT Upper Level Math Section 2

1	Ⓐ Ⓑ Ⓒ Ⓓ Ⓔ	11	Ⓐ Ⓑ Ⓒ Ⓓ Ⓔ	21	Ⓐ Ⓑ Ⓒ Ⓓ Ⓔ
2	Ⓐ Ⓑ Ⓒ Ⓓ Ⓔ	12	Ⓐ Ⓑ Ⓒ Ⓓ Ⓔ	22	Ⓐ Ⓑ Ⓒ Ⓓ Ⓔ
3	Ⓐ Ⓑ Ⓒ Ⓓ Ⓔ	13	Ⓐ Ⓑ Ⓒ Ⓓ Ⓔ	23	Ⓐ Ⓑ Ⓒ Ⓓ Ⓔ
4	Ⓐ Ⓑ Ⓒ Ⓓ Ⓔ	14	Ⓐ Ⓑ Ⓒ Ⓓ Ⓔ	24	Ⓐ Ⓑ Ⓒ Ⓓ Ⓔ
5	Ⓐ Ⓑ Ⓒ Ⓓ Ⓔ	15	Ⓐ Ⓑ Ⓒ Ⓓ Ⓔ	25	Ⓐ Ⓑ Ⓒ Ⓓ Ⓔ
6	Ⓐ Ⓑ Ⓒ Ⓓ Ⓔ	16	Ⓐ Ⓑ Ⓒ Ⓓ Ⓔ		
7	Ⓐ Ⓑ Ⓒ Ⓓ Ⓔ	17	Ⓐ Ⓑ Ⓒ Ⓓ Ⓔ		
8	Ⓐ Ⓑ Ⓒ Ⓓ Ⓔ	18	Ⓐ Ⓑ Ⓒ Ⓓ Ⓔ		
9	Ⓐ Ⓑ Ⓒ Ⓓ Ⓔ	19	Ⓐ Ⓑ Ⓒ Ⓓ Ⓔ		
10	Ⓐ Ⓑ Ⓒ Ⓓ Ⓔ	20	Ⓐ Ⓑ Ⓒ Ⓓ Ⓔ		

SSAT Upper Level Math

Practice Test 2

Section 1

25 questions

Total time for this section: 30 Minutes

You may NOT use a calculator for this test.

1) What is the value of the "9" in number 131.493?
   A. 9 ones
   B. 9 tenths
   C. 9 hundredths
   D. 9 tens
   E. 9 thousandths

2) If $x - 20 = -20$, then $x \times 20 =$?
   A. 0
   B. 10
   C. 20
   D. 40
   E. 60

3) $0.04 \times 13.00 = ?$
   A. 5.2
   B. 52.00
   C. 0.52
   D. 5.02
   E. 0.052

4) If Logan ran 3.5 miles in half an hour, his average speed was?
   A. 2.25 *miles per hour*
   B. 3.5 *miles per hour*
   C. 3.75 *miles per hour*
   D. 4.26 *miles per hour*
   E. 7 *miles per hour*

5) Given the diagram, what is the perimeter of the quadrilateral?
   A. 54
   B. 70
   C. 720
   D. 26740
   E. 55480

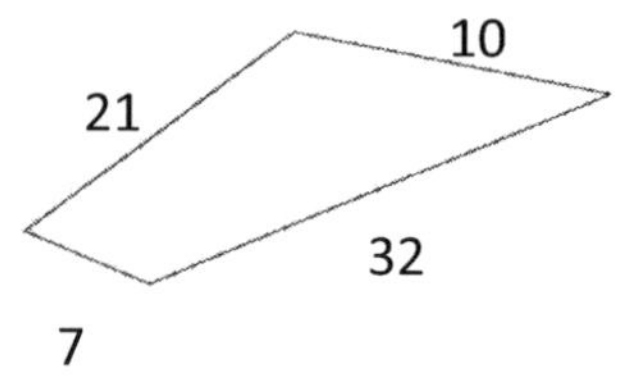

6) A pizza maker has M pounds of flour to make pizzas. After he has used 75 pounds of flour, how much flour is left? The expression that correctly represents the quantity of flour left is:
   A. $75 + M$
   B. $\frac{75}{M}$
   C. $75 - M$
   D. $M - 75$
   E. $75M$

7) Mia plans to buy a bracelet for every one of her 18 friends for their party. There are four bracelets in each pack. How many packs must she buy?
   A. 2
   B. 3
   C. 4
   D. 5
   E. 10

8) The distance between cities A and B is approximately 3,600 miles. If Alice drives an average of 70 miles per hour, how many hours will it take Alice to drive from city A to city B?
   A. $Approximately\ 70\ hours$
   B. $Approximately\ 68\ hours$
   C. $Approximately\ 51 hours$
   D. $Approximately\ 37\ hours$
   E. $Approximately\ 21\ hours$

9) In a classroom of 60 students, 30 are female. What percentage of the class is male?
   A. 54%
   B. 50%
   C. 30%
   D. 26%
   E. 10%

10) A steak dinner at a restaurant costs $9.20. If a man buys a steak dinner for himself and 4 friends, what will the total cost be?
   A. $33
   B. $46
   C. $28
   D. $22.5
   E. 12

11) An employee's rating on performance appraisals for the last three quarters were 93, 40 and 87. If the required yearly average to qualify for the promotion is 97, what rating should the fourth quarter be?
   A. 158
   B. 168
   C. 178
   D. 188
   E. 198

12) Two third of 15 is equal to $\frac{2}{5}$ of what number?

A. 15
B. 25
C. 35
D. 45
E. 55

13) A cruise line ship left Port A and traveled 60 miles due west and then 80 miles due north. At this point, what is the shortest distance from the cruise to port A?

A. $100\ miles$
B. $120\ miles$
C. $130\ miles$
D. $150\ miles$
E. $170\ miles$

14) Last week 25,000 fans attended a football match. This week three times as many bought tickets, but one sixth of them cancelled their tickets. How many are attending this week?

A. 49,000
B. 52,200
C. 62,500
D. 72,500
E. 84,700

15) What is the slope of the line that is perpendicular to the line with equation $8x + y = 14$?

A. $\frac{1}{8}$
B. $-\frac{1}{8}$
C. $\frac{8}{12}$
D. 8
E. -8

16) In 1989, the average worker's income increased \$3,000 per year starting from \$34,000 annual salary. Which equation represents income greater than average? (I = income, x = number of years after 1989)

A. $I > 3{,}000\,x + 34{,}000$
B. $I > \quad 3{,}000\,x + 34{,}000$
C. $I < -3{,}000\,x + 34{,}000$
D. $I < 3{,}000\,x - 34{,}000$
E. $I < 34{,}000\,x + 34{,}000$

17) In the following figure, MN is $50\ cm$. How long is ON?

A. $35\ cm$
B. $30\ cm$
C. $25\ cm$
D. $15\ cm$
E. $5\ cm$

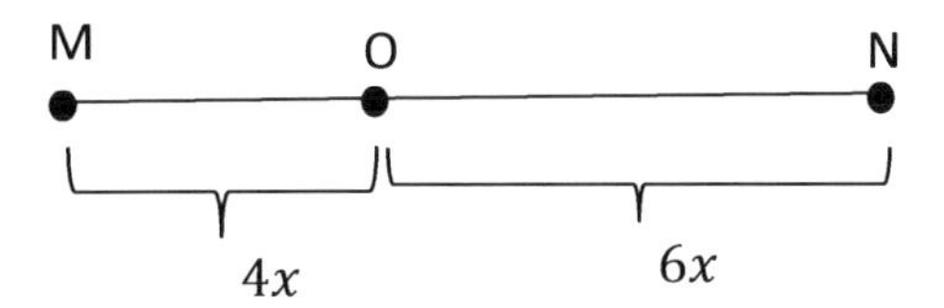

Questions 18 to 20 are based on the following data

The result of a research shows the number of men and women in four cities of a country.

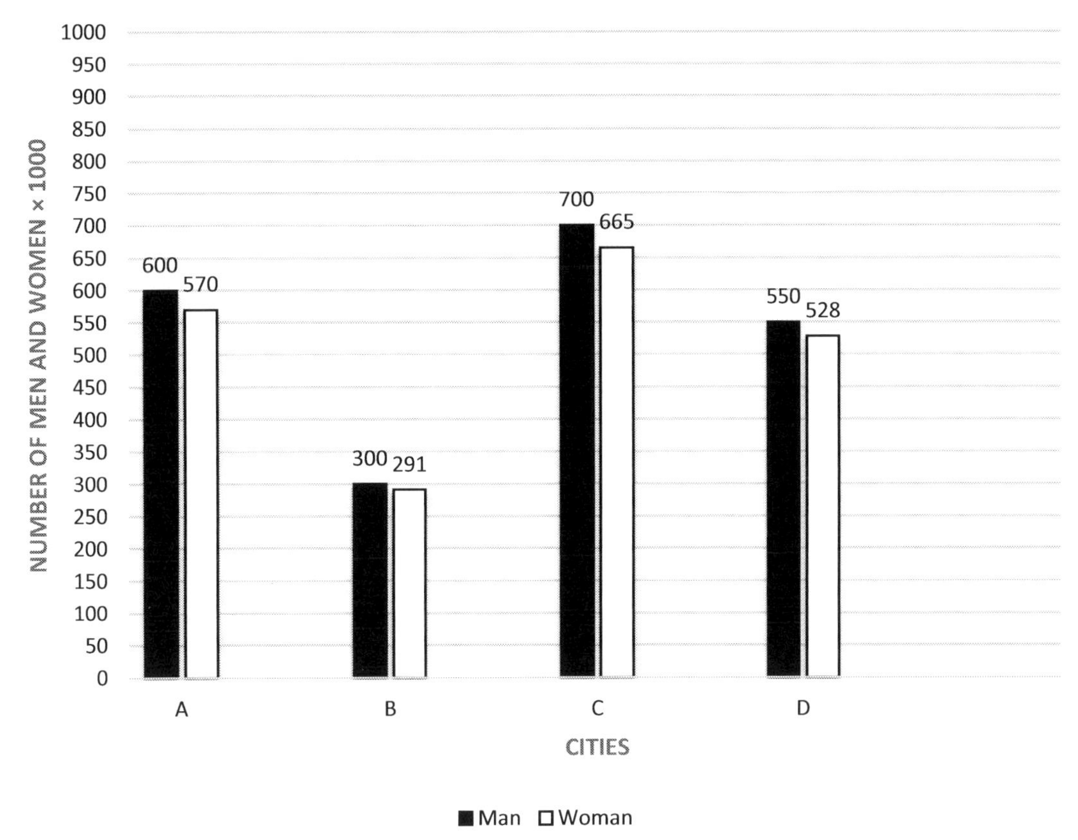

18) How many women should be added to city D until the ratio of women to men will be 1.2?

A. 120
B. 128
C. 132
D. 160
E. 165

19) What's the maximum ratio of woman to man in the four cities?

A. 0.98
B. 0.97
C. 0.96
D. 0.95
E. 0.93

20) What's the ratio of percentage of men in city A to percentage of women in city C?

A. 0.9
B. 0.95
C. 1
D. 1.05
E. 1.5

21) What is the difference of smallest 5–digit number and biggest 5–digit number?

A. $66,666$
B. $6,7899$
C. $8,8888$
D. $8,9999$
E. $9,9999$

22) Solve the following equation for y?

$$\frac{x}{3+4}=\frac{y}{11-8}$$

A. $\frac{3}{5}x$
B. $\frac{3}{7}x$
C. $3x$
D. x
E. $\frac{1}{7}x$

23) $\sqrt[5]{x^{21}}=?$

A. $x^4\sqrt[5]{x}$
B. $20x$
C. x^{11}
D. x^{80}
E. x^4

24) Rectangle A has a length of $10\ cm$ and a width of $6\ cm$, and rectangle B has a length of $6\ cm$ and a width of $4\ cm$, what is the percent of ratio of the perimeter of rectangle B to rectangle A?
A. 10%
B. 20%
C. 62%
D. 75%
E. 143%

25) John traveled $160\ km$ in 4 hours and Alice traveled $190\ km$ in 5 hours. What is the ratio of the average speed of John to average speed of Alice?
A. $2:3$
B. $3:2$
C. $9:5$
D. $6:5$
E. $20:19$

IF YOU FINISH BEFORE TIME IS CALLED, YOU MAY CHECK YOUR WORK ON THIS SECTION ONLY. DO NOT TURN TO ANY OTHER SECTION IN THE TEST.

STOP

SSAT Upper Level Math

Practice Test 2

Section 2

25 questions

Total time for this section: 30 Minutes

You may NOT use a calculator for this test.

1) $0.44 \times 12.8 = ?$
   A. 4.632
   B. 4.965
   C. 5.632
   D. 5.891
   E. 6.695

2) $4\frac{3}{8} \times 5\frac{1}{9} = ?$
   A. $22\frac{1}{36}$
   B. $22\frac{13}{36}$
   C. $23\frac{4}{36}$
   D. $23\frac{13}{36}$
   E. 23

3) Which of the following is a whole number ?
   A. $\frac{3}{2} \times \frac{5}{9}$
   B. $\frac{1}{3} + \frac{1}{4}$
   C. $\frac{40}{6}$
   D. $3.5 + 2$
   E. $3.5 + \frac{4}{8}$

4) 8 cubed is the same as:
   A. 8×8
   B. $8 \times 8 \times 8 \times 8$
   C. 64
   D. 512
   E. 15,807

5) If $\frac{2}{3}$ of a number equal to 16 then $\frac{5}{3}$ of the same number is:
   A. 40
   B. 35
   C. 20
   D. 14
   E. 4

6) A swimming pool holds 3,000 cubic feet of water. The swimming pool is 30 feet long and 10 feet wide. How deep is the swimming pool?
   A. 3 feet
   B. 5 feet
   C. 7 feet
   D. 10 feet
   E. 12 feet

7) We can put 25 colored pencils in each box and we have 450 colored pencils. How many boxes do we need?
   A. 12
   B. 15
   C. 17
   D. 18
   E. 19

8) In the figure below, line A is parallel to line B. What is the value of angle x?
   A. 45 degree
   B. 55 degree
   C. 80 degree
   D. 120 degree
   E. 145 degree

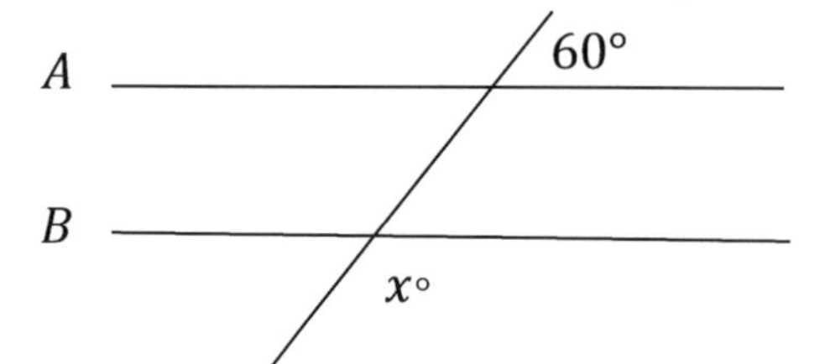

9) A bank is offering 4.5% simple interest on a savings account. If you deposit $13,500, how much interest will you earn in two years?
   A. $420
   B. $750
   C. $6,300
   D. $9,400
   E. $1,215

10) Sophia purchased a sofa for $504. The sofa is regularly priced at $600. What was the percent discount Sophia received on the sofa?
   A. 10%
   B. 12%
   C. 16%
   D. 25%
   E. 30%

11) How long does a 527–miles trip take moving at 62 miles per hour (mph)?

A. $7\ hours$
B. $7\ hours\ and\ 24\ minutes$
C. $8\ hours\ and\ 24\ minutes$
D. $8\ hours\ and\ 30\ minutes$
E. $9\ hours\ and\ 30\ minutes$

12) A construction company is building a wall. The company can build $40\ cm$ of the wall per minute. After 50 minutes construction, $\frac{2}{3}$ of the wall is completed. How high is the wall?

A. $10\ m$
B. $15\ m$
C. $30\ m$
D. $35\ m$
E. $42\ m$

13) When a number is subtracted from 28 and the difference is divided by that number, the result is 3. What is the value of the number?

A. 2
B. 5
C. 7
D. 12
E. 28

14) If car A drives 700 miles in 7 hours and car B drives the same distance in 5 hours, how many miles per hour does car B drive faster than car A?

A. 88 miles per hour
B. 65 miles per hour
C. 40 miles per hour
D. 12 miles per hour
E. 5 miles per hour

15) A company pays its employee $8,000 plus 4% of all sales profit. If x is the number of all sales profit, which of the following represents the employee's revenue?

A. $0.04x$
B. $0.88x - 8{,}000$
C. $0.04x + 8{,}000$
D. $0.88x + 8{,}000$
E. $0.88x$

16) Which of the following shows the numbers in decreasing order?

A. $\frac{1}{5}, \frac{5}{3}, \frac{8}{11}, \frac{2}{3}$
B. $\frac{5}{3}, \frac{8}{11}, \frac{2}{3}, \frac{1}{5}$
C. $\frac{8}{11}, \frac{2}{3}, \frac{5}{3}, \frac{1}{5}$
D. $\frac{2}{3}, \frac{8}{11}, \frac{5}{3}, \frac{1}{5}$
E. None of the above

17) The ratio of boys to girls in a school is $3:2$. If there are 700 students in a school, how many boys are in the school?

A. 550
B. 500
C. 460
D. 420
E. 280

18) $\frac{(8+6)^2}{2} + 6 = ?$

A. 51
B. 80
C. 90
D. 100
E. 104

19) If $y = 5ab + 2b^4$ what is y when $a = 3$ and $= 2$?

A. 34
B. 35
C. 56
D. 62
E. 105

20) The area of a circle is 49π. What is the circumference of the circle?

A. 8π
B. 14π
C. 16π
D. 49π
E. 64π

21) If 80% of x equal to 40% of 20, then what is the value of $(x+7)^2$?

A. 27.27
B. 27
C. 29.01
D. 289
E. $12{,}026$

22) What is the greatest common factor of 18 and 24?

A. 24
B. 18
C. 10
D. 6
E. 4

23) If the interior angles of a quadrilateral are in the ratio $1:2:3:4$, what is the measure of the smallest angle?

A. 36°
B. 72°
C. 108°
D. 144°
E. 180°

24) The length of a rectangle is $\frac{4}{5}$ times its width. If the width is 30, what is the perimeter of this rectangle?

A. 26
B. 58
C. 72
D. 92
E. 108

25) Find $\frac{2}{3}$ of $\frac{3}{4}$ of 160?

A. 80
B. 40
C. 20
D. 4
E. 2

IF YOU FINISH BEFORE TIME IS CALLED, YOU MAY CHECK YOUR WORK ON THIS SECTION ONLY. DO NOT TURN TO ANY OTHER SECTION IN THE TEST.

STOP

SSAT Upper Level Math Practice Test 3

2020 - 2021

Two Parts

Total number of questions: 50

Section 1: 25 questions

Section 2: 25 questions

Total time for two parts: 60 Minutes

SSAT Upper Level Math Practice Test 3 Answer Sheet

Remove (or photocopy) this answer sheet and use it to complete the practice test.

SSAT Upper Level Mathematics Practice Test 3 Answer Sheet

SSAT Upper Level Math Section 1

1	Ⓐ Ⓑ Ⓒ Ⓓ Ⓔ	11	Ⓐ Ⓑ Ⓒ Ⓓ Ⓔ	21	Ⓐ Ⓑ Ⓒ Ⓓ Ⓔ
2	Ⓐ Ⓑ Ⓒ Ⓓ Ⓔ	12	Ⓐ Ⓑ Ⓒ Ⓓ Ⓔ	22	Ⓐ Ⓑ Ⓒ Ⓓ Ⓔ
3	Ⓐ Ⓑ Ⓒ Ⓓ Ⓔ	13	Ⓐ Ⓑ Ⓒ Ⓓ Ⓔ	23	Ⓐ Ⓑ Ⓒ Ⓓ Ⓔ
4	Ⓐ Ⓑ Ⓒ Ⓓ Ⓔ	14	Ⓐ Ⓑ Ⓒ Ⓓ Ⓔ	24	Ⓐ Ⓑ Ⓒ Ⓓ Ⓔ
5	Ⓐ Ⓑ Ⓒ Ⓓ Ⓔ	15	Ⓐ Ⓑ Ⓒ Ⓓ Ⓔ	25	Ⓐ Ⓑ Ⓒ Ⓓ Ⓔ
6	Ⓐ Ⓑ Ⓒ Ⓓ Ⓔ	16	Ⓐ Ⓑ Ⓒ Ⓓ Ⓔ		
7	Ⓐ Ⓑ Ⓒ Ⓓ Ⓔ	17	Ⓐ Ⓑ Ⓒ Ⓓ Ⓔ		
8	Ⓐ Ⓑ Ⓒ Ⓓ Ⓔ	18	Ⓐ Ⓑ Ⓒ Ⓓ Ⓔ		
9	Ⓐ Ⓑ Ⓒ Ⓓ Ⓔ	19	Ⓐ Ⓑ Ⓒ Ⓓ Ⓔ		
10	Ⓐ Ⓑ Ⓒ Ⓓ Ⓔ	20	Ⓐ Ⓑ Ⓒ Ⓓ Ⓔ		

SSAT Upper Level Math Section 2

1	Ⓐ Ⓑ Ⓒ Ⓓ Ⓔ	11	Ⓐ Ⓑ Ⓒ Ⓓ Ⓔ	21	Ⓐ Ⓑ Ⓒ Ⓓ Ⓔ
2	Ⓐ Ⓑ Ⓒ Ⓓ Ⓔ	12	Ⓐ Ⓑ Ⓒ Ⓓ Ⓔ	22	Ⓐ Ⓑ Ⓒ Ⓓ Ⓔ
3	Ⓐ Ⓑ Ⓒ Ⓓ Ⓔ	13	Ⓐ Ⓑ Ⓒ Ⓓ Ⓔ	23	Ⓐ Ⓑ Ⓒ Ⓓ Ⓔ
4	Ⓐ Ⓑ Ⓒ Ⓓ Ⓔ	14	Ⓐ Ⓑ Ⓒ Ⓓ Ⓔ	24	Ⓐ Ⓑ Ⓒ Ⓓ Ⓔ
5	Ⓐ Ⓑ Ⓒ Ⓓ Ⓔ	15	Ⓐ Ⓑ Ⓒ Ⓓ Ⓔ	25	Ⓐ Ⓑ Ⓒ Ⓓ Ⓔ
6	Ⓐ Ⓑ Ⓒ Ⓓ Ⓔ	16	Ⓐ Ⓑ Ⓒ Ⓓ Ⓔ		
7	Ⓐ Ⓑ Ⓒ Ⓓ Ⓔ	17	Ⓐ Ⓑ Ⓒ Ⓓ Ⓔ		
8	Ⓐ Ⓑ Ⓒ Ⓓ Ⓔ	18	Ⓐ Ⓑ Ⓒ Ⓓ Ⓔ		
9	Ⓐ Ⓑ Ⓒ Ⓓ Ⓔ	19	Ⓐ Ⓑ Ⓒ Ⓓ Ⓔ		
10	Ⓐ Ⓑ Ⓒ Ⓓ Ⓔ	20	Ⓐ Ⓑ Ⓒ Ⓓ Ⓔ		

SSAT Upper Level Math

Practice Test 3

Section 1

25 questions

Total time for this section: 30 Minutes

You may NOT use a calculator for this test.

1) A shaft rotates 200 times in 8 seconds. How many times does it rotate in 12 seconds?
   A. 300
   B. 250
   C. 200
   D. 150
   E. 100

2) A school wants to give each of its 23 top students a football ball. If the balls are in boxes of three, how many boxes of balls they need to purchase?
   A. 3
   B. 5
   C. 7
   D. 8
   E. 20

3) If $\frac{25}{A} + 1 = 6$, then $30 + A = ?$
   A. 6
   B. 1
   C. 25
   D. 35
   E. 0

4) How many tiles of $8\ cm^2$ is needed to cover a floor of dimension $7\ cm$ by $24\ cm$?
   A. 6
   B. 12
   C. 21
   D. 24
   E. 36

5) Which of the following statements is correct, according to the graph below?

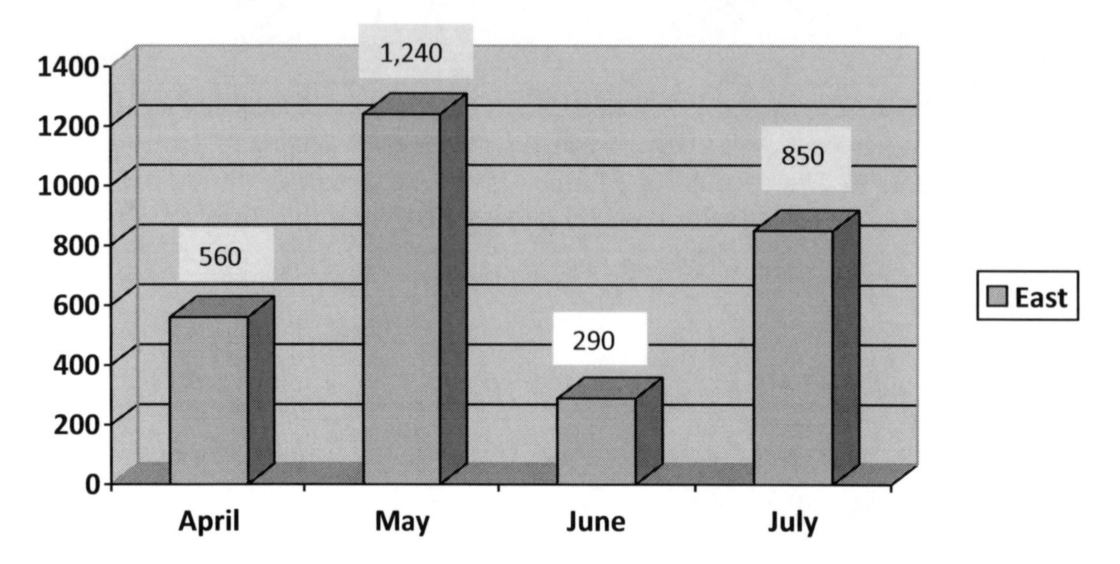

A. Number of books sold in April was twice the number of books sold in July.
B. Number of books sold in July was less than half the number of books sold in May.
C. Number of books sold in June was half the number of books sold in April.
D. Number of books sold in July was equal to the number of books sold in April plus the number of books sold in June.
E. More books were sold in April than in July.

6) $12.124 \div 0.004$?
A. 3.0310
B. 30.310
C. 30,310
D. 3,031
E. 300,310

7) What is the value of the sum of the tens and thousandths in number 5,271.19452?
A. 16
B. 15
C. 14
D. 112
E. 11

8) If 150% of a number is 75, then what is the 80% of that number?
   A. 40
   B. 50
   C. 60
   D. 70
   E. 85

9) Amy and John work in a same company. Last month, both of them received a raise of 20 percent. If Amy earns \$30.00 per hour now and John earns \$28.80, Amy earned how much more per hour than John before their raises?
   A. \$8.25
   B. \$4.25
   C. \$3.00
   D. \$2.25
   E. \$1.00

10) $\frac{1\frac{3}{4}+\frac{1}{3}}{2\frac{1}{2}-\frac{15}{8}}$ is approximately equal to.
   A. 3.33
   B. 3.6
   C. 5.67
   D. 6.33
   E. 6.67

11) If $2 \leq x < 4$, what is the minimum value of the following expression?

$$2x + 1$$

   A. 8
   B. 5
   C. 3
   D. 2
   E. 1

12) If $x \blacksquare y = \sqrt{x^2 + y}$, what is the value of $6 \blacksquare 13$?
   A. $\sqrt{126}$
   B. 7
   C. 4
   D. 3
   E. 2

13) The average weight of 18 girls in a class is $55\ kg$ and the average weight of 32 boys in the same class is $62\ kg$. What is the average weight of all the 50 students in that class?

A. $50\ kg$
B. $59.48\ kg$
C. $61.68\ kg$
D. $61.9\ kg$
E. $62.20\ kg$

14) There are three equal tanks of water. If $\frac{2}{5}$ of a tank contains 250 liters of water, what is the capacity of the three tanks of water together?
A. 1,875 liters
B. 1,200 liters
C. 550 liters
D. 380 liters
E. 200 liters

15) What is the answer of $8.5 \div 0.17$?

A. $\frac{1}{50}$
B. $\frac{1}{5}$
C. 5
D. 50
E. 500

16) Two-kilograms apple and two-kilograms orange cost $26.4. If one-kilogram apple costs $4.2 how much does one-kilogram orange cost?
A. $9
B. $6
C. $5.5
D. $5
E. $4

17) What is the value of x in the following figure?

A. 160
B. 145
C. 125
D. 115
E. 105

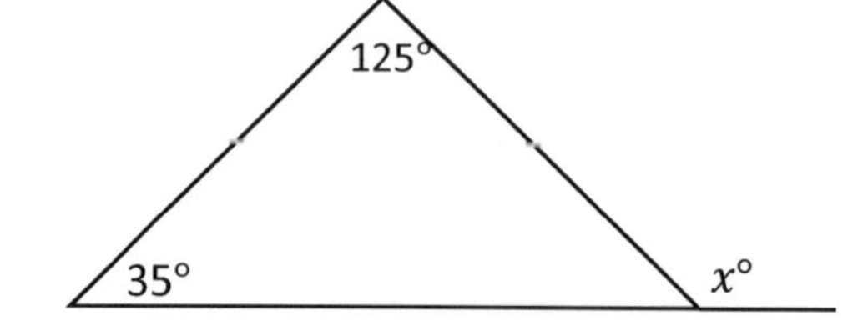

18) Karen is 9 years older than her sister Michelle, and Michelle is 4 years younger than her brother David. If the sum of their ages is 82, how old is Michelle

A. 14
B. 22
C. 23
D. 25
E. 30

19) Michelle and Alec can finish a job together in 50 minutes. If Michelle can do the job by herself in 5 hours, how many minutes does it take Alec to finish the job?

A. 50
B. 60
C. 150
D. 200
E. 220

20) The sum of six different negative integers is -72. If the smallest of these integers is -15, what is the largest possible value of one of the other five integers?

A. -14
B. -10
C. -7
D. -4
E. -1

21) What is the slope of a line that is perpendicular to the line $4x - 2y = 14$?

A. -2
B. $-\frac{1}{2}$
C. 4
D. 12
E. 14

22) A bank is offering 5.5% simple interest on a savings account. If you deposit $\$7{,}000$, how much interest will you earn in five years?

A. $\$360$
B. $\$720$
C. $\$1{,}925$
D. $\$2{,}600$
E. $\$4{,}800$

23) The Jackson Library is ordering some bookshelves. If x is the number of bookshelves the library wants to order, which each costs $\$100$ and there is a one-time delivery charge of $\$900$, which of the following represents the total cost, in dollar, per bookshelf?

A. $100x + 900$

B. $100 + 900x$

C. $\frac{100x+900}{100}$

D. $\frac{100x+900}{x}$

E. $100x - 900$

24) A football team won exactly 60% of the games it played during last session. Which of the following could be the total number of games the team played last season?

A. 49

B. 35

C. 32

D. 16

E. 12

25) The width of a box is one third of its length. The height of the box is one third of its width. If the length of the box is $36\ cm$, what is the volume of the box?

A. $81\ cm^3$

B. $162\ cm^3$

C. $243\ cm^3$

D. $729\ cm^3$

E. $1{,}728\ cm^3$

IF YOU FINISH BEFORE TIME IS CALLED, YOU MAY CHECK YOUR WORK ON THIS SECTION ONLY. DO NOT TURN TO ANY OTHER SECTION IN THE TEST.

STOP

SSAT Upper Level Math

Practice Test 3

Section 2

25 questions

Total time for this section: 30 Minutes

You may NOT use a calculator for this test.

1) There are 11 marbles in the bag A and 19 marbles in the bag B. If the sum of the marbles in both bags will be shared equally between two children, how many marbles bag A has less than the marbles that each child will receive?
   A. 2
   B. 3
   C. 4
   D. 5
   E. 6

2) If the perimeter of the following figure be 26, what is the value of x?
   A. 2
   B. 3
   C. 6
   D. 9
   E. 12

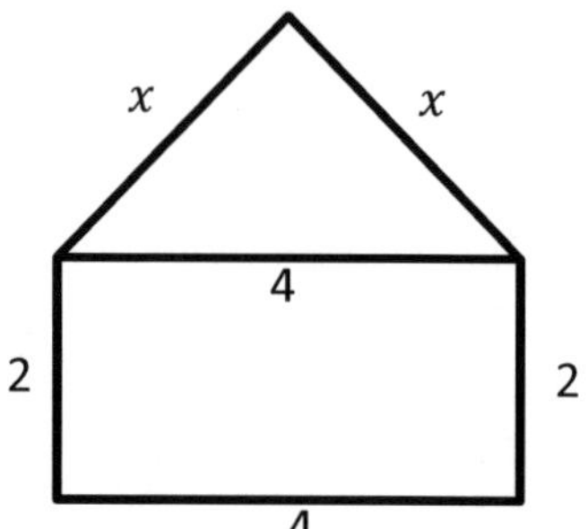

3) When number $92{,}501$ is divided by 305, the result is closest to?
   A. 3
   B. 30
   C. 303
   D. 350
   E. 400

4) If Jason's mark is k more than Alex, and Jason's mark is 15, which of the following can be Alex's mark?
   A. $15 + k$
   B. $k - 15$
   C. $\frac{k}{15}$
   D. $15k$
   E. $15 - k$

5) To paint a wall with the area of $62m^2$, how many liters of paint do we need if each liter of paint is enough to paint a wall with dimension of $62\ cm \times 100\ cm$?
   A. 100
   B. 120
   C. 150
   D. 200
   E. 250

6) The price of a sofa is decreased by 25% to $432. What was its original price?
   A. $480
   B. $520
   C. $576
   D. $600
   E. $800

7) $750 - 8\frac{7}{15} = ?$
   A. $741\frac{7}{15}$
   B. $741\frac{8}{15}$
   C. $743\frac{1}{15}$
   D. $743\frac{8}{15}$
   E. $744\frac{1}{15}$

8) A driver rests one hour and 12 minutes for every 3 hours driving. How many minutes will he rest if he drives 15 hours?
   A. *3 hours and 36 minutest*
   B. *4 hours and 12 minutest*
   C. *4 hours and 45 minutest*
   D. *5 hours and 36 minutest*
   E. *6 hours*

9) Which of the following expression is not equal to 4?
   A. $8 \times \frac{1}{2}$
   B. $20 \times \frac{1}{5}$
   C. $2 \times \frac{4}{2}$
   D. $4 \times \frac{5}{5}$
   E. $4 \times \frac{1}{4}$

10) What is the missing term in the given sequence?

$$2, 3, 5, 8, 12, 17, \_\_, 30$$

   A. 23
   B. 24
   C. 27
   D. 28
   E. 30

Questions 11 to 12 are based on the following graph

A library has 800 books that include Mathematics, Physics, Chemistry, English and History. Use following graph to answer questions 11 to 12.

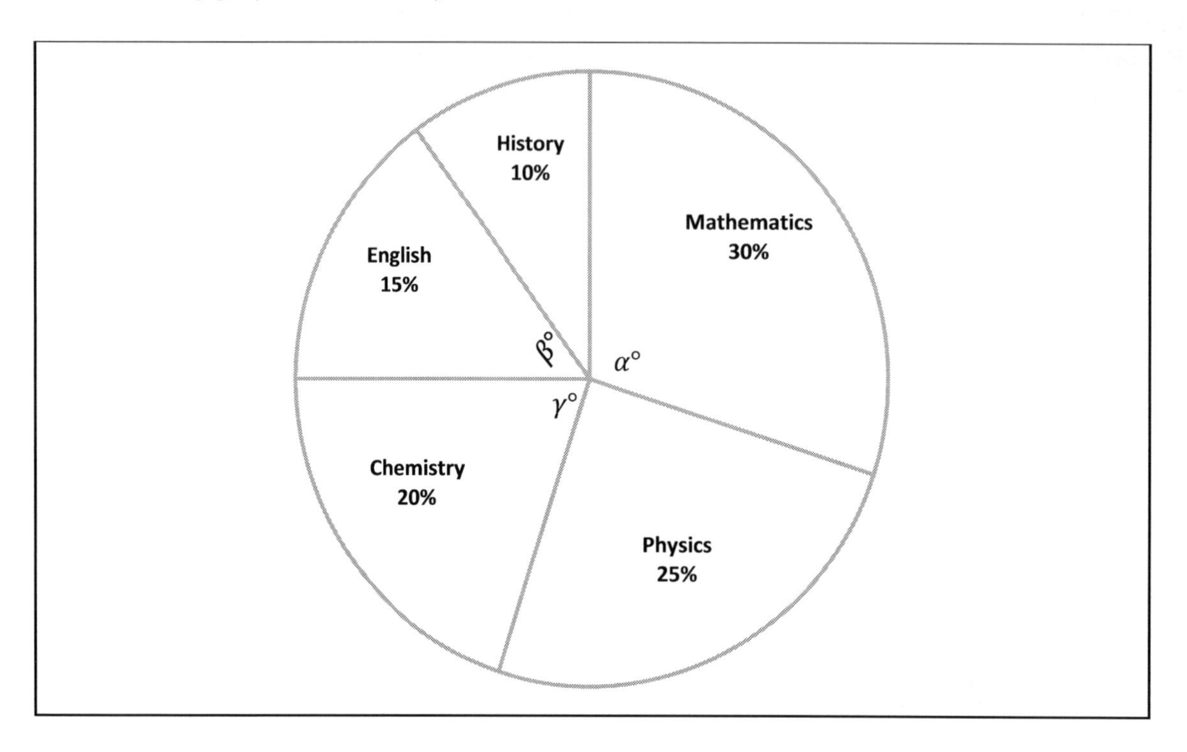

11) What is the product of the number of Mathematics and number of English books?

A. 21,168
B. 28,800
C. 29,460
D. 30,640
E. 35,280

12) What are the values of angle α and β respectively?

A. $90°, 54°$
B. $120°, 36°$
C. $120°, 45°$
D. $108°, 54°$
E. $108°, 45°$

13) The length of a rectangle is 3 times of its width. If the length is 24, what is the perimeter of the rectangle?

A. 24
B. 30
C. 36
D. 48
E. 64

14) If $3y + 2 < 29$, then y could be equal to?

A. 15
B. 12
C. 10.5
D. 9
E. 2.5

15) The capacity of a red box is 20% bigger than the capacity of a blue box. If the red box can hold 36 equal sized books, how many of the same books can the blue box hold?

A. 9
B. 15
C. 21
D. 30
E. 36

16) If $8 + (A \times 12) = 28$, then $A =$

A. $\frac{3}{5}$
B. $\frac{5}{3}$
C. 2
D. $\frac{3}{2}$
E. 12

17) There are 60.2 liters of gas in a car fuel tank. In the first week and second week of April, the car uses 5.28 and 25.9 liters of gas respectively. If the car was park in the third week of April and 10.31 liters of gas will be added to the fuel tank, how many liters of gas are in the fuel tank of the car?

A. 21.41 liters
B. 25.9 liters
C. 27 liters
D. 39.33 liters
E. 71.61 liters

18) If $3x + y = 25$ and $x - z = 18$, what is the value of x?

A. 0
B. 5
C. 10
D. 20
E. it cannot be determined from the information given

19) If 96 is the product of 4 and $8x$, then 96 is divisible by which of the following?

A. $x + 4$
B. $2x - 1$
C. $5x - 3$
D. $x \times 3$
E. $3x + 1$

20) What is the average of circumference of figure A and area of figure B? ($\pi = 3$)

A. 50
B. 53
C. 52
D. 51
E. 50

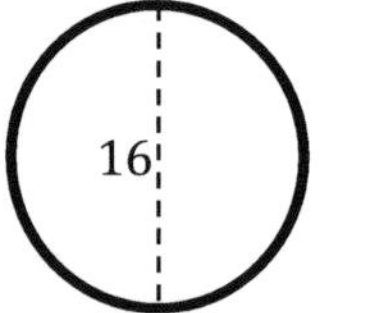

Figure A

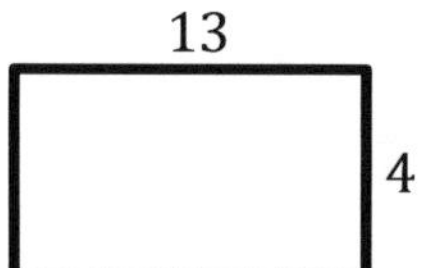

Figure B

21) In the following figure, point Q lies on line n, what is the value of y if $x = 28$?

A. 32
B. 37
C. 42
D. 45
E. 56

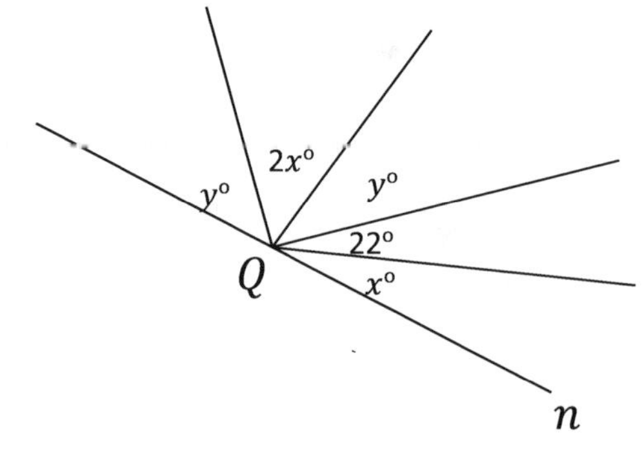

22) Which of the following is closest to $\frac{1}{6}$ of 40?

A. 0.3×6
B. 0.3×5
C. 0.2×30
D. 0.2×35
E. 0.2×39.5

23) A number is chosen at random from 1 to 18. Find the probability of not selecting a composite number. (A composite number is a number that is divisible by itself, 1 and at least one other whole number)

A. $\frac{1}{18}$
B. $\frac{1}{3}$
C. $\frac{7}{18}$
D. 1
E. 0

24) $812 \div 3 = ?$

A. $\frac{800}{3} \times \frac{10}{3} \times \frac{2}{3}$
B. $800 + \frac{10}{3} + \frac{2}{3}$
C. $\frac{800}{3} + \frac{10}{3} + \frac{2}{3}$
D. $\frac{800}{3} \div \frac{10}{3} \div \frac{2}{3}$
E. $\frac{8}{3} + \frac{1}{3} + \frac{2}{3}$

25) If a gas tank can hold 35 gallons, how many gallons does it contain when it is $\frac{2}{5}$ full?

A. 125
B. 62.5
C. 50
D. 14
E. 5

IF YOU FINISH BEFORE TIME IS CALLED, YOU MAY CHECK YOUR WORK ON THIS SECTION ONLY. DO NOT TURN TO ANY OTHER SECTION IN THE TEST.

STOP

SSAT Upper Level Math Practice Test 4

2020 - 2021

Two Parts

Total number of questions: 50

Section 1: 25 questions

Section 2: 25 questions

Total time for two parts: 60 Minutes

SSAT Upper Level Math Practice Test 4 Answer Sheet

Remove (or photocopy) this answer sheet and use it to complete the practice test.

SSAT Upper Level Mathematics Practice Test 4 Answer Sheet

SSAT Upper Level Math Section 1

1	A B C D E	11	A B C D E	21	A B C D E
2	A B C D E	12	A B C D E	22	A B C D E
3	A B C D E	13	A B C D E	23	A B C D E
4	A B C D E	14	A B C D E	24	A B C D E
5	A B C D E	15	A B C D E	25	A B C D E
6	A B C D E	16	A B C D E		
7	A B C D E	17	A B C D E		
8	A B C D E	18	A B C D E		
9	A B C D E	19	A B C D E		
10	A B C D E	20	A B C D E		

SSAT Upper Level Math Section 2

1	A B C D E	11	A B C D E	21	A B C D E
2	A B C D E	12	A B C D E	22	A B C D E
3	A B C D E	13	A B C D E	23	A B C D E
4	A B C D E	14	A B C D E	24	A B C D E
5	A B C D E	15	A B C D E	25	A B C D E
6	A B C D E	16	A B C D E		
7	A B C D E	17	A B C D E		
8	A B C D E	18	A B C D E		
9	A B C D E	19	A B C D E		
10	A B C D E	20	A B C D E		

SSAT Upper Level Math

Practice Test 4

Section 1

25 questions

Total time for this section: 30 Minutes

You may NOT use a calculator for this test.

1) $0.03 \times 12.00 = ?$
   A. 3.6
   B. 36.00
   C. 0.36
   D. 3.06
   E. 0.036

2) If $x - 10 = -10$, then $x \times 3 = ?$
   A. 10
   B. 30
   C. 60
   D. 90
   E. 0

3) What is the value of the "4" in number 131.493?
   A. $4\ ones$
   B. $4\ tenths$
   C. $4\ hundredths$
   D. $4\ tens$
   E. $4\ thousandths$

4) Mia plans to buy a bracelet for every one of her 16 friends for their party. There are three bracelets in each pack. How many packs must she buy?
   A. 3
   B. 4
   C. 5
   D. 6
   E. 10

5) If Logan ran 1.25 miles in 15 minutes, his average speed was?
   A. $1.25\ miles\ per\ hour$
   B. $2.5\ miles\ per\ hour$
   C. $3.75\ miles\ per\ hour$
   D. $5\ miles\ per\ hour$
   E. $10\ miles\ per\ hour$

6) A pizza maker has x pounds of flour to make pizzas. After he has used 55 pounds of flour, how much flour is left? The expression that correctly represents the quantity of flour left is:
   A. $55 + x$
   B. $\frac{55}{x}$
   C. $55 - x$
   D. $x - 55$
   E. $55x$

7) The distance between cities A and B is approximately 2,600 miles. If Alice drives an average of 68 miles per hour, how many hours will it take Alice to drive from city A to city B?
   A. $Approximately\ 41\ hours$
   B. $Approximately\ 38\ hours$
   C. $Approximately\ 29\ hours$
   D. $Approximately\ 27\ hours$
   E. $Approximately\ 21\ hours$

8) Given the diagram, what is the perimeter of the quadrilateral?

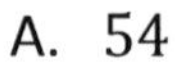

   A. 54
   B. 66
   C. 620
   D. 16,740
   E. 33,480

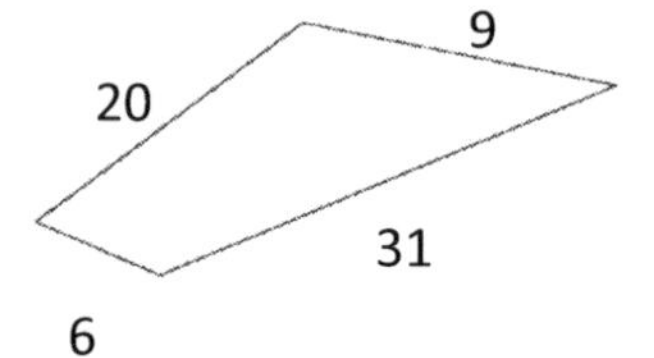

9) In a classroom of 60 students, 42 are female. What percentage of the class is male?
   A. 34%
   B. 22%
   C. 30%
   D. 26%
   E. 15%

10) An employee's rating on performance appraisals for the last three quarters were $92, 88$ and 86. If the required yearly average to qualify for the promotion is 90, what rating should the fourth quarter be?
   A. 91
   B. 92
   C. 93
   D. 94
   E. 95

11) Two third of 18 is equal to $\frac{2}{5}$ of what number?
   A. 12
   B. 20
   C. 30
   D. 60
   E. 90

12) A steak dinner at a restaurant costs $\$8.25$. If a man buys a steak dinner for himself and 3 friends, what will the total cost be?

A. $\$33$
B. $\$27.50$
C. $\$27$
D. $\$21.5$
E. 11

13) Last week 24,000 fans attended a football match. This week three times as many bought tickets, but one sixth of them cancelled their tickets. How many are attending this week?

A. 48,000
B. 54,000
C. 60,000
D. 72,000
E. 84,000

14) What is the slope of the line that is perpendicular to the line with equation $7x + y = 12$?

A. $\frac{1}{7}$
B. $-\frac{1}{7}$
C. $\frac{7}{12}$
D. 7
E. -7

15) A cruise line ship left Port A and traveled 50 miles due west and then 120 miles due north. At this point, what is the shortest distance from the cruise to port A?

A. $70\ miles$
B. $80\ miles$
C. $130\ miles$
D. $160\ miles$
E. $170\ miles$

16) In 1999, the average worker's income increased $\$2,000$ per year starting from $\$24,000$ annual salary. Which equation represents income greater than average? (I = income, x = number of years after 1999)

A. $I > 2,000\,x + 24,000$
B. $I > -2,000\,x + 24,000$
C. $I < -2,000\,x + 24,000$
D. $I < 2,000\,x - 24,000$
E. $I < 24,000\,x + 24,000$

Questions 17 to 19 are based on the following data

The result of a research shows the number of men and women in four cities of a country.

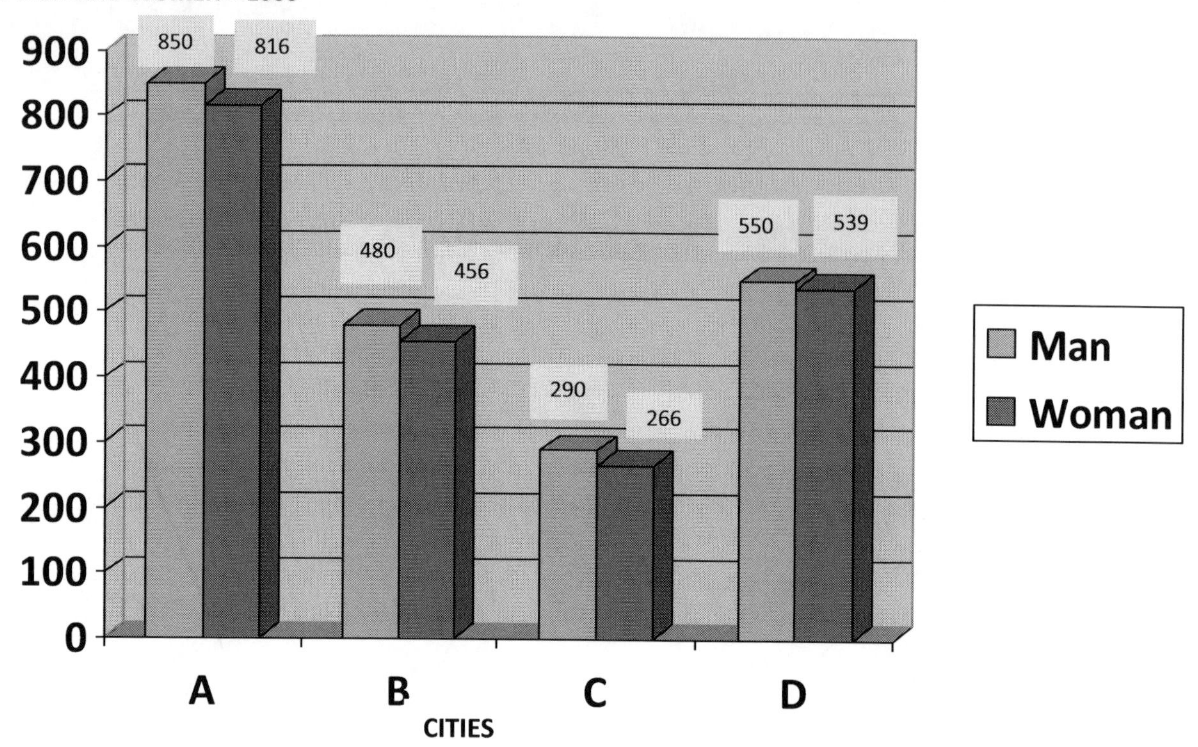

17) What's the maximum ratio of woman to man in the four cities?

A. 0.95
B. 0.96
C. 0.97
D. 0.98
E. 0.99

18) What's the ratio of percentage of men in city A to percentage of women in city C?

A. 0.95
B. 0.98
C. 1
D. 1.07
E. 1.5

19) How many wome n should be added to city D until the ratio of women to men will be 1.4?

A. 187
B. 231
C. 250
D. 289
E. 310

20) In the following figure, MN is $40\ cm$. How long is ON?

A. $25\ cm$
B. $20\ cm$
C. $15\ cm$
D. $10\ cm$
E. $5\ cm$

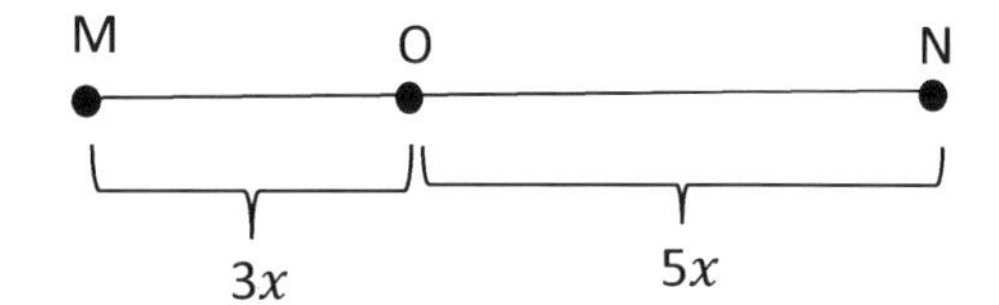

21) Solve the following equation for y?

$$\frac{x}{2+3} = \frac{y}{10-7}$$

A. $\frac{3}{5}x$
B. $\frac{5}{3}x$
C. $3x$
D. $2x$
E. $\frac{1}{2}x$

22) $\sqrt[5]{x^{16}} = ?$

A. $x^3\sqrt[5]{x}$
B. $80x$
C. x^{11}
D. x^{80}
E. x^4

23) John traveled $150\ km$ in 6 hours and Alice traveled $180\ km$ in 4 hours. What is the ratio of the average speed of John to average speed of Alice?

A. $3:2$
B. $2:3$
C. $5:9$
D. $5:6$
E. $11:16$

24) What is the difference of smallest 4–digit number and biggest 4–digit number?
   A. 6,666
   B. 6,789
   C. 8,888
   D. 8,999
   E. 9,999

25) Rectangle A has a length of $8\ cm$ and a width of $4cm$, and rectangle B has a length of $5\ cm$ and a width of $4\ cm$, what is the percent of ratio of the perimeter of rectangle B to rectangle A?
   A. 15%
   B. 25%
   C. 50%
   D. 75%
   E. 133.3%

IF YOU FINISH BEFORE TIME IS CALLED, YOU MAY CHECK YOUR WORK ON THIS SECTION ONLY. DO NOT TURN TO ANY OTHER SECTION IN THE TEST. STOP

SSAT Upper Level Math

Practice Test 4

Section 2

25 questions

Total time for this section: 30 Minutes

You may NOT use a calculator for this test.

1) $5\frac{3}{7} \times 4\frac{1}{5} = ?$
   A. $23\frac{1}{5}$
   B. $23\frac{4}{5}$
   C. $22\frac{4}{5}$
   D. $22\frac{1}{5}$
   E. 21

2) Which of the following is a whole number ?
   A. $\frac{2}{3} \times \frac{9}{5}$
   B. $\frac{1}{2} + \frac{1}{4}$
   C. $\frac{21}{6}$
   D. $2.5 + 1$
   E. $2.5 + \frac{7}{2}$

3) $0.42 \times 11.8 = ?$
   A. 4.956
   B. 4.965
   C. 5.956
   D. 5.965
   E. 5.695

4) Sophia purchased a sofa for $\$530.40$. The sofa is regularly priced at $\$624$. What was the percent discount Sophia received on the sofa?
   A. 12%
   B. 15%
   C. 20%
   D. 25%
   E. 40%

5) If $\frac{2}{5}$ of a number equal to 12 then $\frac{2}{3}$ of the same number is:
   A. 48
   B. 45
   C. 30
   D. 24
   E. 20

6) How long does a 420–miles trip take moving at 50 miles per hour (mph)?
   A. $6\ hours$
   B. $6\ hours\ and\ 24\ minutes$
   C. $8\ hours\ and\ 24\ minutes$
   D. $8\ hours\ and\ 30\ minutes$
   E. $10\ hours\ and\ 30\ minutes$

7) A swimming pool holds $2{,}000$ cubic feet of water. The swimming pool is 25 feet long and 10 feet wide. How deep is the swimming pool?
   A. $2\ feet$
   B. $4\ feet$
   C. $6\ feet$
   D. $7\ feet$
   E. $8\ feet$

8) A bank is offering 3.5% simple interest on a savings account. If you deposit $\$12{,}000$, how much interest will you earn in two years?
   A. $\$420$
   B. $\$840$
   C. $\$4{,}200$
   D. $\$8{,}400$
   E. $\$9{,}000$

9) In the figure below, line A is parallel to line B. What is the value of angle x?
   A. $35 degree$
   B. $45\ degree$
   C. $90\ degree$
   D. $100\ degree$
   E. $145\ degree$

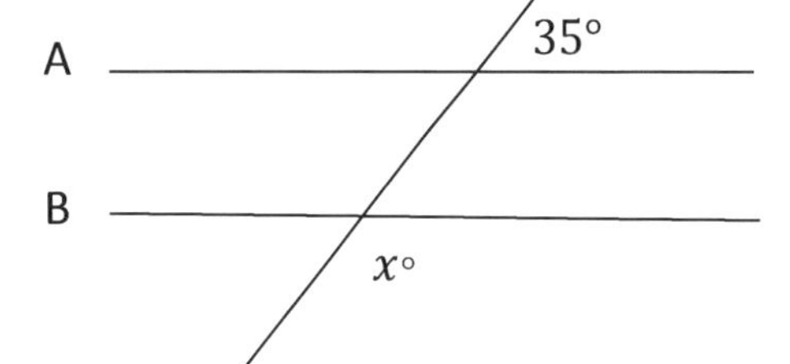

10) We can put 24 colored pencils in each box and we have 408 colored pencils. How many boxes do we need?
   A. 13
   B. 14
   C. 15
   D. 16
   E. 17

11) A construction company is building a wall. The company can build $30\ cm$ of the wall per minute. After 40 minutes construction, $\frac{3}{4}$ of the wall is completed. How high is the wall?

A. $9\ m$
B. $12\ m$
C. $16\ m$
D. $18\ m$
E. $20\ m$

12) 7 cubed is the same as:
A. 7×7
B. $7 \times 7 \times 7 \times 7$
C. 14
D. 343
E. $16{,}807$

13) When a number is subtracted from 24 and the difference is divided by that number, the result is 3. What is the value of the number?

A. 2
B. 4
C. 6
D. 12
E. 24

14) If car A drives 600 miles in 8 hours and car B drives the same distance in 7.5 hours, how many miles per hour does car B drive faster than car A?
A. 80 miles per hour
B. 75 miles per hour
C. 15 miles per hour
D. 10 miles per hour
E. 5 miles per hour

15) The ratio of boys to girls in a school is $2:3$. If there are 600 students in a school, how many boys are in the school?

A. 540
B. 360
C. 300
D. 280
E. 240

16) $\frac{(7+5)^2}{4} + 5 = ?$

A. 41
B. 42
C. 43
D. 44
E. 45

17) If $y = 4ab + 3b^3$, what is y when $a = 2$ and $b = 3$?

A. 24
B. 31
C. 36
D. 51
E. 105

18) A company pays its employee $7,000 plus 2% of all sales profit. If x is the number of all sales profit, which of the following represents the employee's revenue?

A. $0.02x$
B. $0.98x - 7{,}000$
C. $0.02x + 7{,}000$
D. $0.98x + 7{,}000$
E. $0.09x$

19) Which of the following shows the numbers in increasing order?

A. $\frac{2}{3}, \frac{5}{7}, \frac{8}{11}, \frac{3}{4}$
B. $\frac{5}{7}, \frac{3}{4}, \frac{8}{11}, \frac{2}{3}$
C. $\frac{8}{11}, \frac{3}{4}, \frac{5}{7}, \frac{2}{3}$
D. $\frac{5}{7}, \frac{8}{11}, \frac{3}{4}, \frac{2}{3}$
E. None of the above

20) The area of a circle is $64\,\pi$. What is the circumference of the circle?

A. $8\,\pi$
B. $12\,\pi$
C. $16\,\pi$
D. $32\,\pi$
E. $64\,\pi$

21) If 60% of x equal to 30% of 20, then what is the value of $(x+5)^2$?

A. 25.25
B. 26
C. 26.01
D. 225
E. $11{,}025$

22) What is the greatest common factor of 36 and 54?

A. 28
B. 24
C. 18
D. 12
E. 8

23) The length of a rectangle is $\frac{5}{4}$ times its width. If the width is 16, what is the perimeter of this rectangle?

A. 36
B. 48
C. 72
D. 144
E. 180

24) Find $\frac{1}{4}$ of $\frac{2}{5}$ of 120?

A. 16
B. 12
C. 8
D. 4
E. 2

25) If the interior angles of a quadrilateral are in the ratio $1:4:6:7$, what is the measure of the smallest angle?

A. 18°
B. 20°
C. 72°
D. 120°
E. 140°

IF YOU FINISH BEFORE TIME IS CALLED, YOU MAY CHECK YOUR WORK ON THIS SECTION ONLY. DO NOT TURN TO ANY OTHER SECTION IN THE TEST.

STOP

SSAT Upper Level Math Practice Test 5

2020 - 2021

Two Parts

Total number of questions: 50

Section 1: 25 questions

Section 2: 25 questions

Total time for two parts: 60 Minutes

SSAT Upper Level Math Practice Test 5 Answer Sheet

Remove (or photocopy) this answer sheet and use it to complete the practice test.

SSAT Upper Level Mathematics Practice Test 5 Answer Sheet

SSAT Upper Level Practice Section 1

#	Choices	#	Choices	#	Choices
1	Ⓐ Ⓑ Ⓒ Ⓓ Ⓔ	11	Ⓐ Ⓑ Ⓒ Ⓓ Ⓔ	21	Ⓐ Ⓑ Ⓒ Ⓓ Ⓔ
2	Ⓐ Ⓑ Ⓒ Ⓓ Ⓔ	12	Ⓐ Ⓑ Ⓒ Ⓓ Ⓔ	22	Ⓐ Ⓑ Ⓒ Ⓓ Ⓔ
3	Ⓐ Ⓑ Ⓒ Ⓓ Ⓔ	13	Ⓐ Ⓑ Ⓒ Ⓓ Ⓔ	23	Ⓐ Ⓑ Ⓒ Ⓓ Ⓔ
4	Ⓐ Ⓑ Ⓒ Ⓓ Ⓔ	14	Ⓐ Ⓑ Ⓒ Ⓓ Ⓔ	24	Ⓐ Ⓑ Ⓒ Ⓓ Ⓔ
5	Ⓐ Ⓑ Ⓒ Ⓓ Ⓔ	15	Ⓐ Ⓑ Ⓒ Ⓓ Ⓔ	25	Ⓐ Ⓑ Ⓒ Ⓓ Ⓔ
6	Ⓐ Ⓑ Ⓒ Ⓓ Ⓔ	16	Ⓐ Ⓑ Ⓒ Ⓓ Ⓔ		
7	Ⓐ Ⓑ Ⓒ Ⓓ Ⓔ	17	Ⓐ Ⓑ Ⓒ Ⓓ Ⓔ		
8	Ⓐ Ⓑ Ⓒ Ⓓ Ⓔ	18	Ⓐ Ⓑ Ⓒ Ⓓ Ⓔ		
9	Ⓐ Ⓑ Ⓒ Ⓓ Ⓔ	19	Ⓐ Ⓑ Ⓒ Ⓓ Ⓔ		
10	Ⓐ Ⓑ Ⓒ Ⓓ Ⓔ	20	Ⓐ Ⓑ Ⓒ Ⓓ Ⓔ		

SSAT Upper Level Practice Section 2

#	Choices	#	Choices	#	Choices
1	Ⓐ Ⓑ Ⓒ Ⓓ Ⓔ	11	Ⓐ Ⓑ Ⓒ Ⓓ Ⓔ	21	Ⓐ Ⓑ Ⓒ Ⓓ Ⓔ
2	Ⓐ Ⓑ Ⓒ Ⓓ Ⓔ	12	Ⓐ Ⓑ Ⓒ Ⓓ Ⓔ	22	Ⓐ Ⓑ Ⓒ Ⓓ Ⓔ
3	Ⓐ Ⓑ Ⓒ Ⓓ Ⓔ	13	Ⓐ Ⓑ Ⓒ Ⓓ Ⓔ	23	Ⓐ Ⓑ Ⓒ Ⓓ Ⓔ
4	Ⓐ Ⓑ Ⓒ Ⓓ Ⓔ	14	Ⓐ Ⓑ Ⓒ Ⓓ Ⓔ	24	Ⓐ Ⓑ Ⓒ Ⓓ Ⓔ
5	Ⓐ Ⓑ Ⓒ Ⓓ Ⓔ	15	Ⓐ Ⓑ Ⓒ Ⓓ Ⓔ	25	Ⓐ Ⓑ Ⓒ Ⓓ Ⓔ
6	Ⓐ Ⓑ Ⓒ Ⓓ Ⓔ	16	Ⓐ Ⓑ Ⓒ Ⓓ Ⓔ		
7	Ⓐ Ⓑ Ⓒ Ⓓ Ⓔ	17	Ⓐ Ⓑ Ⓒ Ⓓ Ⓔ		
8	Ⓐ Ⓑ Ⓒ Ⓓ Ⓔ	18	Ⓐ Ⓑ Ⓒ Ⓓ Ⓔ		
9	Ⓐ Ⓑ Ⓒ Ⓓ Ⓔ	19	Ⓐ Ⓑ Ⓒ Ⓓ Ⓔ		
10	Ⓐ Ⓑ Ⓒ Ⓓ Ⓔ	20	Ⓐ Ⓑ Ⓒ Ⓓ Ⓔ		

SSAT Upper Level Math

Practice Test 5

Section 1

25 questions

Total time for this section: 30 Minutes

You may NOT use a calculator for this test.

1) The number 40.5 is 1,000 times greater than which of the following numbers?
   A. 0.405

   B. 0.0405

   C. 0.0450

   D. 0.00405

   E. 0.000405

2) When $P + Q = 12$ and $3R + Q = 12$, what is the value of R?
   A. 12
   B. 2
   C. 0
   D. -2
   E. It cannot be determined from the information given.

3) From the figure, which of the following must be true? (figure not drawn to scale)
   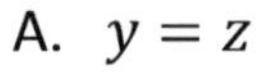
   A. $y = z$
   B. $y = 5x$
   C. $y \geq x$
   D. $y + 4x = z$
   E. $y > x$

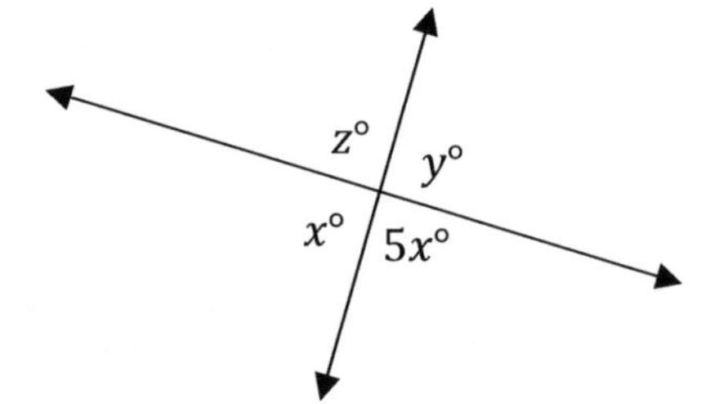

4) Which is the correct statement?
   A. $\frac{3}{4} > 0.8$
   B. $10\% = \frac{2}{5}$
   C. $3 < \frac{5}{2}$
   D. $\frac{5}{6} > 0.8$
   E. None of them above

5) When 40% of 60 is added to 12% of 600, the resulting number is:
   A. 24
   B. 72
   C. 96
   D. 140
   E. 180

6) What is the value of the sum of the tens and thousandths in number 2,517.19458?
   A. 16
   B. 11
   C. 9
   D. 14
   E. 5

7) Jack earns $616 for his first 44 hours of work in a week and is then paid 1.5 times his regular hourly rate for any additional hours. This week, Jack needs $826 to pay his rent, bills and other expenses. How many hours must he work to make enough money in this week?
   A. 40
   B. 48
   C. 50
   D. 53
   E. 54

8) $12.124 \div 0.002$?
   A. 6.0620
   B. 60.620
   C. 606.20
   D. 6,062.0
   E. 600,620

9) $\frac{1\frac{5}{4}+\frac{1}{3}}{2\frac{1}{2}-\frac{15}{8}}$ is approximately equal to.
   A. 4.133
   B. 4.6
   C. 5.67
   D. 6.33
   E. 6.67

10) If 150% of a number is 75, then what is the 90% of that number?
   A. 45
   B. 50
   C. 60
   D. 70
   E. 85

11) If $y = (-3x^3)^2$, which of the following expressions is equal to y?

A. $-6x^5$
B. $-6x^6$
C. $6x^5$
D. $9x^5$
E. $9x^6$

12) There are three equal tanks of water. If $\frac{2}{5}$ of a tank contains 200 liters of water, what is the capacity of the three tanks of water together?

A. 1,500 liters
B. 500 liters
C. 240 liters
D. 80 liters
E. 200 liters

13) What is the answer of $7.5 \div 0.15$?

A. $\frac{1}{50}$
B. $\frac{1}{5}$
C. 5
D. 50
E. 500

14) The average weight of 18 girls in a class is 60 kg and the average weight of 32 boys in the same class is 62 kg. What is the average weight of all the 50 students in that class?

A. 60 kg
B. 61.28 kg
C. 61.68 kg
D. 61.9 kg
E. 62.20 kg

15) If $1 \le x < 4$, what is the minimum value of the following expression?

$$2x + 1$$

A. 8
B. 5
C. 3
D. 2
E. 1

16) What is the value of x in the following figure?

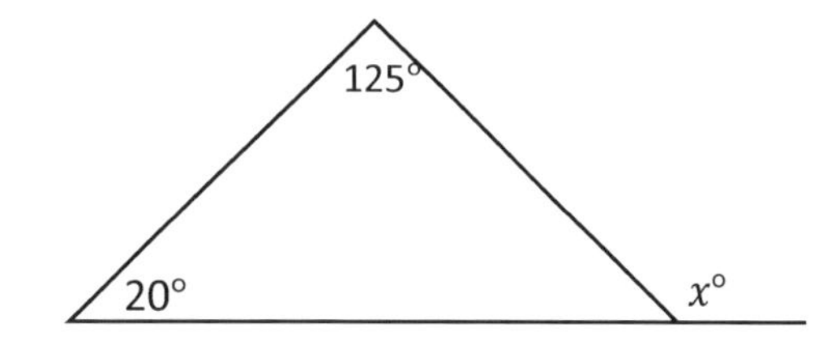

A. 150
B. 145
C. 125
D. 115
E. 105

17) Michelle and Alec can finish a job together in 100 minutes. If Michelle can do the job by herself in 5 hours, how many minutes does it take Alec to finish the job?
A. 120
B. 150
C. 180
D. 200
E. 220

18) The sum of six different negative integers is -70. If the smallest of these integers is -15, what is the largest possible value of one of the other five integers?
A. -14
B. -10
C. -5
D. -4
E. -1

19) David's current age is 42 years, and Ava's current age is 6 years old. In how many years David's age will be 4 times Ava's age?
A. 4
B. 6
C. 8
D. 10
E. 14

20) 5 less than twice a positive integer is 73. What is the integer?
A. 39
B. 41
C. 42
D. 44
E. 50

21) What is the slope of a line that is perpendicular to the line $x - 2y = 12$?
   A. -2
   B. $-\frac{1}{2}$
   C. 4
   D. 12
   E. 14

22) A cruise line ship left Port A and traveled 80 miles due west and then 150 miles due north. At this point, what is the shortest distance from the cruise to port A?
   A. $70\ miles$
   B. $80\ miles$
   C. $150\ miles$
   D. $170\ miles$
   E. $230\ miles$

23) A football team won exactly 80% of the games it played during last session. Which of the following could be the total number of games the team played last season?
   A. 49
   B. 35
   C. 32
   D. 16
   E. 12

24) The width of a box is one third of its length. The height of the box is one third of its width. If the length of the box is $27\ cm$, what is the volume of the box?
   A. $81\ cm^3$
   B. $162\ cm^3$
   C. $243\ cm^3$
   D. $729\ cm^3$
   E. $1{,}880\ cm^3$

25) What is the equivalent temperature of $104°F$ in Celsius?

$$C = \frac{5}{9}(F - 32)$$

   A. 32
   B. 40
   C. 48
   D. 52
   E. 64

IF YOU FINISH BEFORE TIME IS CALLED, YOU MAY CHECK YOUR WORK ON THIS SECTION ONLY. DO NOT TURN TO ANY OTHER SECTION IN THE TEST. **STOP**

SSAT Upper Level Math

Practice Test 5

Section 2

25 questions

Total time for this section: 30 Minutes

You may NOT use a calculator for this test.

1) There are 11 marbles in the bag A and 17 marbles in the bag B. If the sum of the marbles in both bags will be shared equally between two children, how many marbles bag A has less than the marbles that each child will receive?
   A. 2
   B. 3
   C. 4
   D. 5
   E. 6

2) When number 91,501 is divided by 305, the result is closest to?
   A. 3
   B. 30
   C. 300
   D. 350
   E. 400

3) If Jason's mark is k more than Alex, and Jason's mark is 16, which of the following can be Alex's mark?
   A. $16 + k$
   B. $k - 16$
   C. $\frac{k}{16}$
   D. $16k$
   E. $16 - k$

4) To paint a wall with the area of $36m^2$, how many liters of paint do we need if each liter of paint is enough to paint a wall with dimension of $72\ cm \times 100\ cm$?
   A. 50
   B. 100
   C. 150
   D. 200
   E. 250

5) If the perimeter of the following figure be 20, what is the value of x?
   A. 2
   B. 3
   C. 6
   D. 9
   E. 12

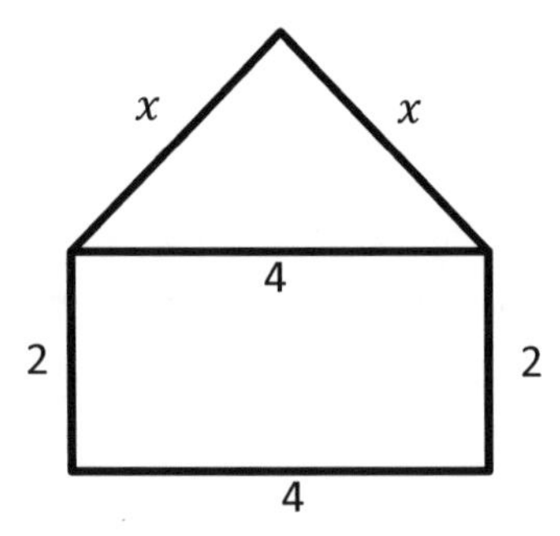

6) $750 - 7\frac{7}{15} = ?$

A. $742\frac{7}{15}$
B. $742\frac{8}{15}$
C. $743\frac{1}{15}$
D. $743\frac{8}{15}$
E. $744\frac{1}{15}$

7) Which of the following expression is not equal to 5?

A. $10 \times \frac{1}{2}$
B. $25 \times \frac{1}{5}$
C. $2 \times \frac{5}{2}$
D. $6 \times \frac{5}{6}$
E. $5 \times \frac{1}{5}$

8) What is the missing term in the given sequence?

$$2, 3, 5, 8, 12, 17, 23, \_\_, 38$$

A. 24
B. 26
C. 27
D. 28
E. 30

9) A driver rests one hour and 12 minutes for every 4 hours driving. How many minutes will he rest if he drives 20 hours?

A. $3\ hours\ and\ 36\ minutest$
B. $4\ hours\ and\ 12\ minutest$
C. $4\ hours\ and\ 45\ minutest$
D. $5\ hours\ and\ 36\ minutest$
E. $6\ hours$

10) The price of a sofa is decreased by 25% to \$420. What was its original price?

A. \$480
B. \$520
C. \$560
D. \$600
E. \$800

11) x is $y\%$ of what number?

A. $\frac{100x}{y}$
B. $\frac{100y}{x}$
C. $\frac{x}{100y}$
D. $\frac{y}{100x}$
E. $\frac{xy}{100}$

12) 120 is equal to

A. $20 - (4 \times 10) + (6 \times 30)$
B. $\left(\frac{11}{8} \times 72\right) + \left(\frac{125}{5}\right)$
C. $\left(\left(\frac{30}{4} + \frac{13}{2}\right) \times 7\right) - \frac{11}{2} + \frac{110}{4}$
D. $(2 \times 10) + (50 \times 1.5) + 15$
E. $\frac{481}{6} + \frac{121}{3}$

13) If $3y + 5 < 29$, then y could be equal to?

A. 15
B. 12
C. 10.5
D. 8
E. 2.5

14) The capacity of a red box is 20% bigger than the capacity of a blue box. If the red box can hold 30 equal sized books, how many of the same books can the blue box hold?

A. 9
B. 15
C. 21
D. 25
E. 30

15) Find the perimeter of following shape.

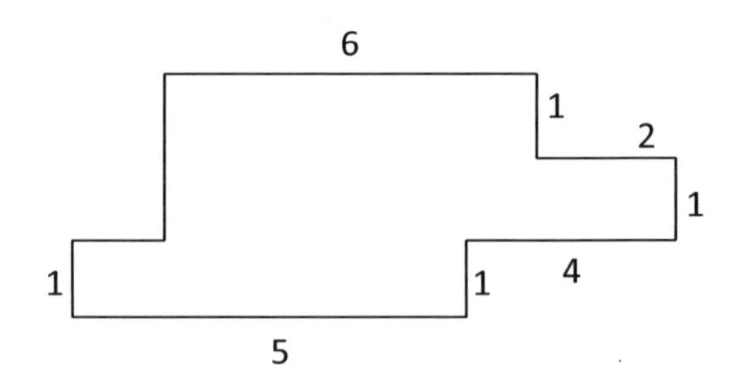

A. 21
B. 22
C. 23
D. 24
E. 25

16) There are 50.2 liters of gas in a car fuel tank. In the first week and second week of April, the car uses 5.82 and 25.9 liters of gas respectively. If the car was park in the third week of April and 10.31 liters of gas will be added to the fuel tank, how many liters of gas are in the fuel tank of the car?
   A. 21.41
   B. 25.9
   C. 27
   D. 28.79
   E. 71.61

17) If $3x + y = 25$ and $x - z = 14$, what is the value of x?
   A. 0
   B. 5
   C. 10
   D. 20
   E. It cannot be determined from the information given

18) What is the average of circumference of figure A and area of figure B? ($\pi = 3$)
   A. 54
   B. 53
   C. 52
   D. 51
   E. 50

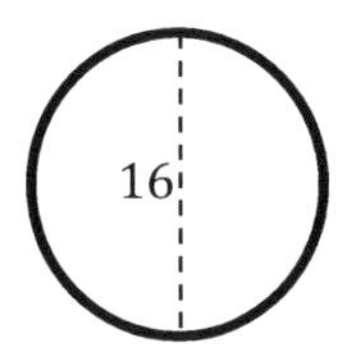

Figure A

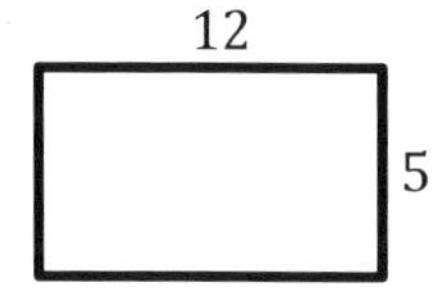

Figure B

19) If $a \times b$ is divisible by 3, which of the following expression must also be divisible by 3?
   A. $a + b$
   B. $3a - b$
   C. $a - 3b + 1$
   D. $\frac{a}{b}$
   E. $4 \times a \times b$

20) In the following figure, ABCD is a rectangle, and E and F are points on AD and DC, respectively. The area of ΔBED is 16, and the area of ΔBDF is 18. What is the perimeter of the rectangle?
   A. 20
   B. 22
   C. 32
   D. 40
   E. 44

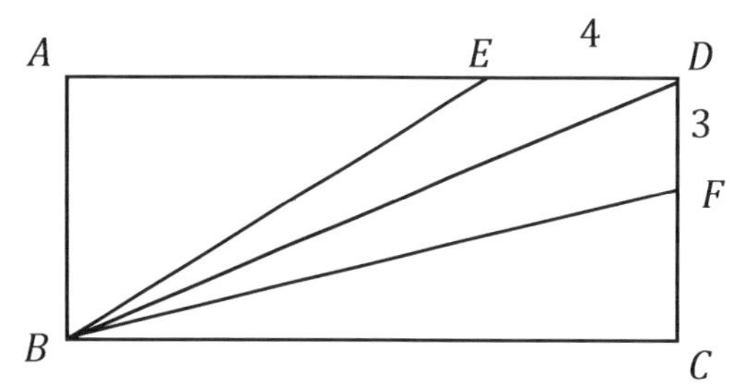

21) If the area of the following trapezoid is 100, what is the perimeter of the trapezoid?

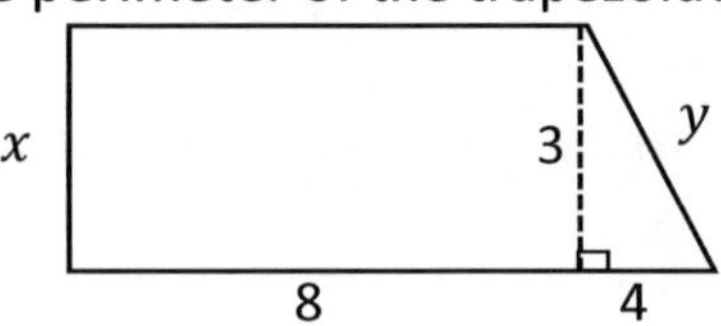

A. 25
B. 35
C. 45
D. 55
E. 65

22) In the following figure, ABCD is a rectangle. If $a = \sqrt{3}$, and $b = 2a$, find the area of the shaded region. (the shaded region is a trapezoid)

4

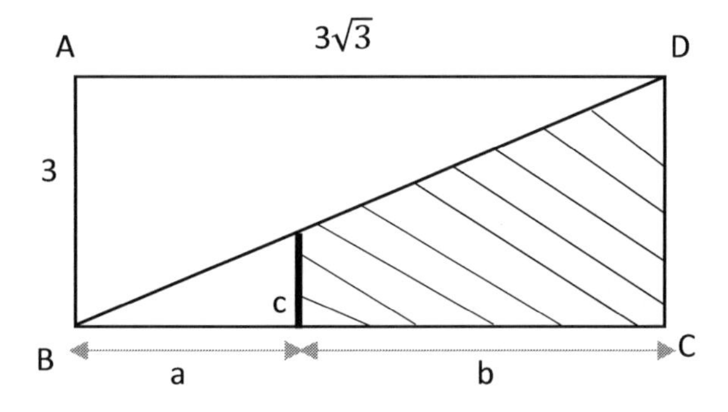

A. 2
B. $\sqrt{3}$
C. $2\sqrt{3}$
D. $4\sqrt{3}$

23) $712 \div 3 =?$

A. $\frac{700}{3} \times \frac{10}{3} \times \frac{2}{3}$
B. $700 + \frac{10}{3} + \frac{2}{3}$
C. $\frac{700}{3} + \frac{10}{3} + \frac{2}{3}$
D. $\frac{700}{3} \div \frac{10}{3} \div \frac{2}{3}$
E. $\frac{7}{3} + \frac{1}{3} + \frac{2}{3}$

24) If a gas tank can hold 25 gallons, how many gallons does it contain when it is $\frac{2}{5}$ full?

A. 125
B. 62.5
C. 50
D. 10
E. 5

25) Which of the following could be the value of x if $\frac{5}{9} + x > 2$?

A. $\frac{1}{2}$
B. $\frac{3}{5}$
C. $\frac{4}{5}$
D. $\frac{4}{3}$
E. $\frac{5}{3}$

IF YOU FINISH BEFORE TIME IS CALLED, YOU MAY CHECK YOUR WORK ON THIS SECTION ONLY. DO NOT TURN TO ANY OTHER SECTION IN THE TEST.

STOP

SSAT Upper Level Math Practice Test Answer Keys

Now, it's time to review your results to see where you went wrong and what areas you need to improve.

SSAT Upper Level Math Practice Test 1								SSAT Upper Level Math Practice Test 2							
Section 1				Section 2				Section 1				Section 2			
1	**C**	16	**A**	1	**A**	16	**E**	1	**C**	16	**A**	1	**C**	16	**B**
2	**B**	17	**C**	2	**A**	17	**E**	2	**A**	17	**B**	2	**B**	17	**D**
3	**A**	18	**A**	3	**E**	18	**E**	3	**C**	18	**C**	3	**E**	18	**E**
4	**D**	19	**B**	4	**E**	19	**C**	4	**E**	19	**B**	4	**D**	19	**D**
5	**D**	20	**B**	5	**E**	20	**D**	5	**B**	20	**D**	5	**A**	20	**B**
6	**C**	21	**B**	6	**B**	21	**E**	6	**D**	21	**D**	6	**D**	21	**D**
7	**D**	22	**A**	7	**E**	22	**B**	7	**D**	22	**B**	7	**D**	22	**D**
8	**B**	23	**D**	8	**A**	23	**B**	8	**C**	23	**A**	8	**D**	23	**A**
9	**A**	24	**D**	9	**E**	24	**C**	9	**B**	24	**C**	9	**E**	24	**E**
10	**C**	25	**A**	10	**E**	25	**C**	10	**B**	25	**E**	10	**C**	25	**A**
11	**C**			11	**E**			11	**B**			11	**D**		
12	**B**			12	**D**			12	**B**			12	**C**		
13	**D**			13	**B**			13	**A**			13	**C**		
14	**D**			14	**D**			14	**C**			14	**C**		
15	**D**			15	**D**			15	**A**			15	**C**		

SSAT Upper Level Math Practice Test 3

Section 1				Section 2			
1	**A**	16	**A**	1	**C**	16	**B**
2	**D**	17	**A**	2	**D**	17	**D**
3	**D**	18	**C**	3	**C**	18	**E**
4	**C**	19	**B**	4	**E**	19	**C**
5	**D**	20	**C**	5	**A**	20	**A**
6	**D**	21	**B**	6	**C**	21	**B**
7	**E**	22	**C**	7	**B**	22	**D**
8	**A**	23	**D**	8	**E**	23	**C**
9	**E**	24	**B**	9	**E**	24	**C**
10	**A**	25	**E**	10	**A**	25	**D**
11	**B**			11	**B**		
12	**B**			12	**D**		
13	**B**			13	**E**		
14	**A**			14	**E**		
15	**D**			15	**D**		

SSAT Upper Level Math Practice Test 4

Section 1				Section 2			
1	**C**	16	**A**	1	**C**	16	**A**
2	**E**	17	**D**	2	**E**	17	**E**
3	**B**	18	**D**	3	**A**	18	**C**
4	**D**	19	**B**	4	**B**	19	**A**
5	**D**	20	**A**	5	**E**	20	**C**
6	**D**	21	**A**	6	**C**	21	**D**
7	**B**	22	**A**	7	**E**	22	**C**
8	**B**	23	**C**	8	**B**	23	**C**
9	**C**	24	**D**	9	**E**	24	**B**
10	**D**	25	**D**	10	**E**	25	**B**
11	**C**			11	**C**		
12	**A**			12	**D**		
13	**C**			13	**C**		
14	**A**			14	**E**		
15	**C**			15	**E**		

SSAT Upper Level Math Practice Test 5

Section 1				Section 2			
1	**B**	16	**B**	1	**B**	16	**D**
2	**E**	17	**B**	2	**C**	17	**E**
3	**D**	18	**C**	3	**E**	18	**A**
4	**D**	19	**B**	4	**A**	19	**E**
5	**C**	20	**A**	5	**C**	20	**D**
6	**E**	21	**A**	6	**B**	21	**B**
7	**E**	22	**D**	7	**E**	22	**E**
8	**D**	23	**B**	8	**E**	23	**C**
9	**A**	24	**D**	9	**E**	24	**D**
10	**A**	25	**B**	10	**C**	25	**E**
11	**E**			11	**A**		
12	**A**			12	**C**		
13	**D**			13	**E**		
14	**B**			14	**D**		
15	**C**			15	**D**		

SSAT Upper Level Math Practice Test

Answers and Explanations

SSAT Upper Level Mathematics Practice Test 1 Section 1

1) Choice C is correct

Number of packs equal to: $\frac{22}{4} \cong 5.5$, therefore, the school must purchase 6 packs.

2) Choice B is correct

First create a proportion: $\frac{240}{12} = \frac{x}{20}$, Number of rotates in 20 second equals to: $\frac{240 \times 20}{12} = 400$

3) Choice A is correct

$x = 30 + 120 = 150$

4) Choice D is correct

$14.125 \div 0.005 = \frac{\frac{14,125}{1,000}}{\frac{5}{1,000}} = \frac{14,125}{5} = 2,825$

5) Choice D is correct

The area of the floor is: $5\ cm \times 20\ cm = 100\ cm^2$, the number of tiles needed =

$$100 \div 5 = 20$$

6) Choice C is correct

$\frac{30}{A} + 1 = 7 \rightarrow \frac{30}{A} = 7 - 1 = 6 \rightarrow 30 = 6A \rightarrow A = \frac{30}{6} = 5, 30 + A = 30 + 5 = 35$

7) Choice D is correct

The digit in tens place is 1. The digit in the thousandths place is 6. Therefore; $1 + 6 = 7$

8) Choice B is correct

The amount of money that Jack earns for one hour: $\frac{\$720}{45} = \$16$

Number of additional hours that he needs to work in order to make enough money is: $\frac{\$936 - \$720}{1.5 \times \$16} = 9$, number of total hours Jack must work is: $45 + 9 = 54$

9) Choice A is correct

First, find the number. Let x be the number. Write the equation and solve for x.

50% of a number is 85, then: $0.5 \times x = 85 \rightarrow x = 85 \div 0.5 = 170$

20% of 170 is: $0.2 \times 170 = 34$

10) Choice C is correct

A. Number of books sold in April is: 380

Number of books sold in July is: $760 \rightarrow \frac{380}{760} = \frac{38}{76} = \frac{1}{2}$

B. Number of books sold in July is: 760

Half the number of books sold in May is: $\frac{1140}{2} = 570 \rightarrow 760 > 570$

C. Number of books sold in June is: 190

Half the number of books sold in April is: $\frac{380}{2} = 190 \rightarrow 190 = 190$

D. $380 + 190 = 570 < 760$

E. $380 < 760$

11) Choice C is correct

$6 \blacksquare 28 = \sqrt{6^2 + 28 =} \sqrt{36 + 28} = \sqrt{64} = 8$

12) Choice B is correct

$2 \leq x < 6 \rightarrow$ Multiply all sides of the inequality by 3. Then:

$2 \times 3 \leq 3 \times x < 6 \times 3 \rightarrow 6 \leq 3x < 18$

Add 1 to all sides. Then: $\rightarrow 6 + 1 \leq 3x + 1 < 18 + 1 \rightarrow \ 7 \leq 3x + 1 < 19$

Minimum value of $3x + 1$ is 7.

13) Choice D is correct

$0.90 \div 0.015 = \frac{0.90}{0.015} = \frac{\frac{90}{100}}{\frac{15}{1,000}} = \frac{90 \times 1,000}{15 \times 100} = \frac{90}{15} \times \frac{1,000}{100} = 6 \times 10 = 60$

14) Choice D is correct

$\frac{1\frac{4}{3}+\frac{1}{4}}{2\frac{1}{2}-\frac{17}{8}} = \frac{\frac{7}{3}+\frac{1}{4}}{\frac{5}{2}-\frac{17}{8}} = \frac{\frac{28+3}{12}}{\frac{20-17}{8}} = \frac{\frac{31}{12}}{\frac{3}{8}} = \frac{31 \times 8}{12 \times 3} = \frac{31 \times 2}{3 \times 3} = \frac{62}{9} \cong 6.88$

15) Choice D is correct

Let x be the capacity of one tank. Then, $\frac{2}{5}x = 300 \rightarrow x = \frac{300 \times 5}{2} = 750$ Liters

The amount of water in four tanks is equal to: $4 \times 750 = 3{,}000$ Liters

16) Choice A is correct

Use the information provided in the question to draw the shape.

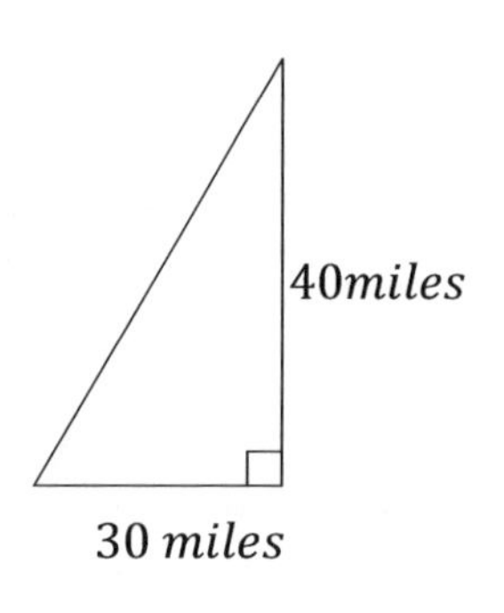

Use Pythagorean Theorem: $\mathrm{a}^2 + \mathrm{b}^2 = \mathrm{c}^2$

$30^2 + 40^2 = \mathrm{c}^2 \Rightarrow 900 + 1{,}600 = \mathrm{c}^2 \Rightarrow 2500 = \mathrm{c}^2 \Rightarrow \mathrm{c} = 50$ miles

17) Choice C is correct

$Average = \frac{sum\ of\ terms}{number\ of\ terms},$

The sum of the weight of all girls is: $20 \times 55 = 1{,}100\ kg$, The sum of the weight of all boys is: $42 \times 82 = 3{,}444\ kg$, The sum of the weight of all students is: $1{,}100 + 3{,}444 = 4{,}544kg$

The average weight of the 62 students: $\frac{4,544}{62} = 73.29\ kg$

18) Choice A is correct

Let x be the cost of one-kilogram orange, then: $2x + (2 \times 5.2) = 28.4 \rightarrow$

$$2x + 10.4 = 28.4 \rightarrow 2x = 28.4 - 10.4 \rightarrow 2x = 18 \rightarrow x = \frac{18}{2} = \$9$$

19) Choice B is correct

Let's review the choices provided.

A. 4. In 4 years, David will be 48 and Ava will be 8.48 is not 5 times 8.
B. 6. In 6 years, David will be 50 and Ava will be 10. 50 is 5 times 10!
C. 8. In 8 years, David will be 52 and Ava will be 12. 52 is not 5 times 12.
D. 10. In 10 years, David will be 54 and Ava will be 14. 54 is not 5 times 14.
E.14. In 14 years, David will be 58 and Ava will be 18.58 is not 5 times 18.

20) Choice B is correct

Let b be the amount of time Alec can do the job, (change 2.5 hours to 150 minutes) then:

$\frac{1}{a} + \frac{1}{b} = \frac{1}{50} \rightarrow \frac{1}{150} + \frac{1}{b} = \frac{1}{50} \rightarrow \frac{1}{b} = \frac{1}{50} - \frac{1}{150} = \frac{2}{150} = \frac{1}{75}$, Then: b = 75 minutes

21) Choice B is correct

The smallest number is -16. To find the largest possible value of one of the other five integers, we need to choose the smallest possible integers for four of them. *Let* x be the largest number. Then: $-80 = (-16) + (-15) + (-14) + (-13) + (-12) + x \rightarrow$

$-80 = -70 + x, \rightarrow x = -80 + 70 = -10$

22) Choice A is correct

The equation of a line in slope intercept form is: $y = mx + b$, Solve for y.

$$2x - 4y = 24 \Rightarrow -4y = 24 - 2x \Rightarrow y = (24 - 2x) \div (-4) \Rightarrow y = \frac{1}{2}x - 6$$

The slope is $\frac{1}{2}$. The slope of the line perpendicular to this line is:

$$m_1 \times m_2 = -1 \Rightarrow \frac{1}{2} \times m_2 = -1 \Rightarrow m_2 = -2$$

23) Choice D is correct

If the length of the box is 24, then the width of the box is one third of it, 8, and the height of the box is 4 (half of the width). The volume of the box is:

$$V = (length)(width)(height) = (24)(8)(4) = 768\ cm^3$$

24) Choice D is correct

Choices A, B, C and E are incorrect because 70% of each of the numbers is non-whole number.

A. 59, 70% of $59 = 0.70 \times 59 = 41.3$
B. 45, 70% of $45 = 0.70 \times 45 = 31.5$
C. 72, 70% of $72 = 0.70 \times 72 = 50.4$
D. 20, 70% of $20 = 0.70 \times 20 = 14$
E. 11, 70% of $11 = 0.70 \times 11 = 7.7$

25) Choice A is correct

The amount of money *for* x bookshelf is: $200x$, Then, the total cost of all bookshelves is equal to: $200x + 600$, The total cost, in dollar, per bookshelf is: $\frac{Total\ cost}{number\ of\ items} = \frac{200x+600}{x}$

SSAT Upper Level Mathematics Practice Test 1 Section 2

1) Choice A is correct

$\frac{14+18}{2} = \frac{32}{2} = 16$ Then, $16 - 14 = 2$

2) Choice A is correct

Alex's mark is F less than Jason's mark. Then, from the choices provided Alex's mark can only be $18 - F$.

3) Choice E is correct

$\frac{81602}{240} \cong 340.0083 \cong 340$

4) Choice E is correct

Let x be the original price. If the price of the sofa is decreased by 50% to $\$530$, then:
50% of $x = 530 \Rightarrow 0.50x = 530 \Rightarrow x = 530 \div 0.50 = 1{,}060$

5) Choice E is correct

Let's review the choices provided:

A. $x = 3 \rightarrow$ The perimeter of the figure is: $3 + 5 + 3 + 3 + 3 = 17 \neq 33$
B. $x = 4 \rightarrow$ The perimeter of the figure is: $3 + 5 + 3 + 4 + 4 = 19 \neq 33$
C. $x = 6 \rightarrow$ The perimeter of the figure is: $3 + 5 + 3 + 6 + 6 = 23 \neq 33$
D. $x = 8 \rightarrow$ The perimeter of the figure is: $3 + 5 + 3 + 8 + 8 = 27 \neq 33$
E. $x = 11 \rightarrow$ The perimeter of the figure is: $3 + 5 + 3 + 11 + 11 = 33 = 33$

6) Choice B is correct

The Area that one liter of paint is required: $80cm \times 95cm = 7{,}600cm^2$

Remember: $1\ m^2 = 10{,}000\ cm^2\ (100 \times 100 = 10{,}000), then, 7{,}600cm^2 = 0.76\ m^2$

Number of liters of paint we need: $\frac{57}{0.76} = 75$ liters

7) Choice E is correct

Let's review the choices provided:

A. $12 \times \frac{1}{2} = \frac{12}{2} = 6 = 6$
B. $24 \times \frac{1}{4} = \frac{24}{4} = 6 = 6$
C. $2 \times \frac{6}{2} = \frac{12}{2} = 6 = 6$
D. $5 \times \frac{6}{5} = \frac{30}{5} = 6 = 6$
E. $6 \times \frac{1}{6} = \frac{6}{6} = 1 \neq 6$

8) Choice A is correct

$760 - 9\frac{8}{14} = (759 - 9) + \left(\frac{14}{14} - \frac{8}{14}\right) = 750\frac{3}{7}$

9) Choice E is correct

Find the difference of each pairs of numbers: $3, 4, 6, 9, 13, 18, 24, \_\_, 39$

The difference of 3 and 4 is 1, 4 and 6 is 2, 6 and 9 is 3, 9 and 13 is 4, 13 and 18 is 5, 18 and 24 is 6, 24 and next number should be 7. The number is $24 + 7 = 31$

10) Choice E is correct

Number of times that the driver rests $= \frac{24}{3} = 8$, Driver's rest time $=$

$1\ hour\ and\ 15\ minutes = 75\ minutes$, Then, $8 \times 75\ minutes = 600\ minutes$

$1\ hour = 60\ minutes = 600\ minutes = 10\ hours$

11) Choice E is correct

$5y + 5 < 30 \rightarrow 5y < 30 - 5 \rightarrow 5y < 25 \rightarrow y < 5$, the only choice that is less than 5 is E.

12) Choice D is correct

Since, E is the midpoint of AB, then the area of all triangles DAE, DEF, CFE and CBE are equal. Let x be the area of one of the triangle, then: $4x = 160 \rightarrow x = 40$

The area of $DEC = 2x = 2(40) = 80$

13) Choice B is correct

Number of Mathematics book: $0.3 \times 840 = 252$, Number of English books: $0.15 \times 840 = 126$, Product of number of Mathematics and number of English books: $252 \times 126 = 31{,}752$

14) Choice D is correct

The angle α is: $0.3 \times 360 = 108°$, The angle β is: $0.15 \times 360 = 54°$

15) Choice D is correct

The capacity of a red box is 20% bigger than the capacity of a blue box and it can hold 60 books. Therefore, we want to find a number that 20% bigger than that number is 60. Let x be that number. Then: $1.20 \times x = 60$, Divide both sides of the equation by 1.2. Then:

$x = \frac{60}{1.20} = 50$

16) Choice E is correct

We have two equations and three unknown variables, therefore x cannot be obtained.

17) Choice E is correct

$x + 2 = 2 + 2 + 2 \rightarrow x = 4$

$y + 7 + 3 = 6 + 5 \rightarrow y + 10 = 11 \rightarrow y = 1$

Then, the perimeter is:

$2 + 6 + 2 + 5 + 2 + 3 + 2 + 7 + 4 + 1 = 34$

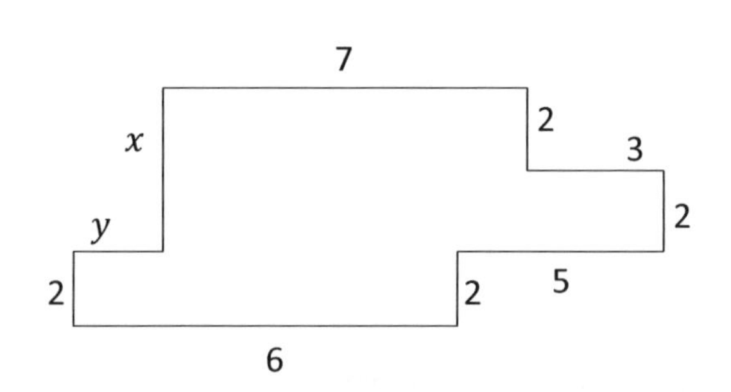

18) Choice E is correct

Amount of available petrol in tank: $60.4 - 4.86 - 23.9 + 11.22 = 42.86$ liters

19) Choice C is correct

Let put some values for a and b. If $a = 8$ and $b = 2 \rightarrow a \times b = 16 \rightarrow \frac{16}{4} = 8 \rightarrow 16$ is divisible by 4 then;

A. $2a - 5b = (2 \times 8) - (5 \times 2) = 6$ is not divisible by 4
B. $3a - b = (3 \times 8) - 2 = 24 - 2 = 22$ is not divisible by 4

If $a = 10$ and $b = 4 \rightarrow a \times b = 40 \rightarrow \frac{40}{4} = 10$ is not divisible by 4 then;

C. $2a \times 3b = 20 \times (3 \times 4) = 20 \times 12 = 240$ is divisible by 4
D. $\frac{a}{b} = \frac{10}{4}$ is not divisible by 4
E. $\frac{a \times b}{3} = \frac{10 \times 4}{3} = 13.33$

For choice C, if you try any other numbers for a and b, you will get the same result.

20) Choice D is correct
Let's review the choices provided:

A. $x = \frac{1}{3} \rightarrow \frac{6}{8} + \frac{1}{3} = \frac{18+8}{24} = \frac{26}{24} \cong 1.083 < 2$
B. $x = \frac{3}{5} \rightarrow \frac{6}{8} + \frac{3}{5} = \frac{30+24}{40} = \frac{54}{40} \cong 1.35 < 2$
C. $x = \frac{6}{5} \rightarrow \frac{6}{8} + \frac{6}{5} = \frac{30+48}{40} = \frac{78}{40} \cong 1.95 < 2$
D. $x = \frac{4}{3} \rightarrow \frac{6}{8} + \frac{4}{3} = \frac{18+32}{24} = \frac{50}{24} \cong 2.08 > 2$
E. $x = \frac{2}{3} \rightarrow \frac{6}{8} + \frac{2}{3} = \frac{18+16}{24} = \frac{34}{24} \cong 1.41 < 2$
Only choice D is correct.

21) Choice E is correct
$\frac{3}{4} \times 20 = \frac{60}{4} = 15$

22) Choice B is correct
The angles on a straight line add up to 180 degrees. Let's review the choices provided:

A. $y = 10 \rightarrow x + 25 + y + 2x + y = 35 + 25 + 10 + 2(35) + 10 = 150 \neq 180$
B. $y = 25 \rightarrow x + 25 + y + 2x + y = 35 + 25 + 25 + 2(35) + 25 = 180$
C. $y = 30 \rightarrow x + 25 + y + 2x + y = 35 + 25 + 30 + 2(35) + 30 = 190 \neq 180$
D. $y = 40 \rightarrow x + 25 + y + 2x + y = 35 + 25 + 40 + 2(35) + 40 = 210 \neq 180$
E. $y = 50 \rightarrow x + 25 + y + 2x + y = 35 + 25 + 50 + 2(35) + 50 = 230 \neq 180$

23) Choice B is correct
Set of numbers that are not composite between 1 and 20: $A = \{2, 3, 5, 7, 11, 13, 17, 19\}$

$$Probability = \frac{number\ of\ desired\ outcomes}{number\ of\ total\ outcomes} = \frac{8}{20} = \frac{2}{5}$$

24) Choice C is correct
$615 \div 4 = \frac{615}{4} = \frac{600+10+5}{4} = \frac{600}{4} + \frac{10}{4} + \frac{5}{4}$

25) Choice C is correct

Perimeter of figure A is: $2\pi r = 2\pi \frac{20}{2} = 20\pi = 20 \times 3 = 60$

Area of figure B is: $5 \times 12 = 60$, $Average = \frac{60+60}{2} = \frac{120}{2} = 60$

SSAT Upper Level Mathematics Practice Test 2 Section 1

1) Choice C is correct
Digit 9 is in the hundredths place.

2) Choice A is correct
$x - 20 = -20 \rightarrow x = -20 + 20 \rightarrow x = 0$, Then; $x \times 20 = 0 \times 20 = 0$

3) Choice C is correct
$0.04 \times 13.00 = \frac{4}{100} \times \frac{13}{1} = \frac{52}{100} = 0.52$

4) Choice E is correct
His average speed was: $\frac{3.5}{0.5} = 7$ miles per hour

5) Choice B is correct
The perimeter of the quadrilateral is: $7 + 21 + 10 + 32 = 70$

6) Choice D is correct
The amount of flour is: $M - 75$

7) Choice D is correct
Number of packs needed equals to: $\frac{18}{4} \cong 4.5$, Then Mia must purchase 5 packs.

8) Choice C is correct
The time it takes to drive from city A to city B is: $\frac{3{,}600}{70} = 51.42$, It's approximately 51 hours.

9) Choice B is correct
Number of males in the classroom is: $60 - 30 = 30$

Then, the percentage of males in the classroom is: $\frac{30}{60} \times 100 = 0.5 \times 100 = 50\%$

10) Choice B is correct
For one person the total cost is: \$9.20, Therefore, for five persons, the total cost is:

$$5 \times \$9.20 = \$46$$

11) Choice B is correct

Let x be the fourth quarter rate, then: $\frac{93+40+87+x}{4} = 97$, Multiply both sides of the above equation by 4. Then: $4 \times \left(\frac{93+40+87+x}{4}\right) = 4 \times 97 \rightarrow 93 + 40 + 87 + x = 388 \rightarrow 220 + x = 388, \rightarrow x = 388 - 220 = 168$

12) Choice B is correct

Let x be the number. Write the equation and solve for x. $\frac{2}{3} \times 15 = 10 \rightarrow 10 = \frac{2}{5}x$, multiply both sides of the equation by $\frac{5}{2}$, then: $10 \times \frac{5}{2} = \frac{2}{5}x \times \frac{5}{2} \rightarrow x = 25$

13) Choice A is correct

Use the information provided in the question to draw the shape.

Use Pythagorean Theorem: $a^2 + b^2 = c^2$

$60^2 + 80^2 = c^2 \Rightarrow 3{,}600 + 6{,}400 = c^2 \Rightarrow 10{,}000 = c^2 \Rightarrow c = 100$ *miles*

80 *miles*

Port A

60 *miles*

14) Choice C is correct

Three times of 25,000 is 75,000. One sixth of them cancelled their tickets.

One sixth of 75,000 equals 12,500 ($\frac{1}{6} \times 75{,}000 = 12{,}500$).

62,500 ($75{,}000 - 12{,}500 = 62{,}500$) fans are attending this week

15) Choice A is correct

The equation of a line in slope intercept form is: $y = mx + b$, Solve for y: $8x + y = 14 \Rightarrow y = -8x + 14$,The slope of this line is -8.The slope of the line perpendicular to this line is:

$m_1 \times m_2 = -1 \Rightarrow -8 \times m_2 = -1 \Rightarrow m_2 = \frac{1}{8}$

16) Choice A is correct

Let x be the number of years. Therefore, \$3,000 per year equals $3{,}000x$. Starting from \$34,000 annual salary means you should add that amount to $3{,}000x$. Income more than that is: $I > 3{,}000x + 34{,}000$

17) Choice B is correct

The length of MN is equal to: $4x + 6x = 10x$, Then: $10x = 50 \rightarrow x = \frac{50}{10} = 5$

The length of ON is equal to: $6x = 6 \times 5 = 30\ cm$

18) Choice C is correct

Let the number of women should be added to city D be x, then:

$$\frac{528 + x}{550} = 1.2 \rightarrow 528 + x = 550 \times 1.2 = 660 \rightarrow x = 132$$

19) Choice B is correct

Ratio of women to men in city A: $\frac{570}{600} = 0.95$

Ratio of women to men in city B: $\frac{291}{300} = 0.97$

Ratio of women to men in city C: $\frac{665}{700} = 0.95$

Ratio of women to men in city D: $\frac{528}{550} = 0.96$

0.97 is the maximum ratio of woman to man in the four cities.

20) Choice D is correct

Percentage of men in city $= \frac{600}{1,170} \times 100 = 51.28\%$, Percentage of women in city $C = \frac{665}{1,365} \times 100 = 48.72\%$, Percentage of men in city A to percentage of women in city $C = \frac{51.28}{48.72} = 1.05$

21) Choice D is correct

Smallest 5–digit number is 10,000, and biggest 5–digit number is 99,999. The difference is: 89,999

22) Choice B is correct

$\frac{x}{3+4} = \frac{y}{11-8} \rightarrow \frac{x}{7} = \frac{y}{3} \rightarrow 7y = 3x \rightarrow y = \frac{3}{7}x$

23) Choice A is correct

$\sqrt[5]{x^{21}} = \sqrt[5]{x^{20} \times x} = \sqrt[5]{x^{20}} \times \sqrt[5]{x} = x^{\frac{20}{5}} \times \sqrt[5]{x} = x^4 \sqrt[5]{x}$

24) Choice C is correct

Perimeter of rectangle A is equal to: $2 \times (10 + 6) = 2 \times 16 = 32$

Perimeter of rectangle B is equal to: $2 \times (6 + 4) = 2 \times 10 = 20$

Therefore: $\frac{20}{32} \times 100 = 0.625 \times 100 = 62.5\% \cong 62\%$

25) Choice E is correct

The average speed of John is: $160 \div 4 = 40\ km$, The average speed of Alice is: $190 \div 5 = 38\ km$, Write the ratio and simplify. $40 : 38 \Rightarrow 20 : 19$

SSAT Upper Level Mathematics Practice Test 2 Section 2

1) Choice C is correct

$0.44 \times 12.8 = \frac{44}{100} \times \frac{128}{10} = \frac{44 \times 128}{100 \times 10} = \frac{5,632}{1,000} = 5.632$

2) Choice B is correct

$4\frac{3}{8} \times 5\frac{1}{9} = \frac{35}{8} \times \frac{46}{9} = \frac{35 \times 46}{8 \times 9} = \frac{1,610}{72} = \frac{805}{36} = 22\frac{13}{36}$

3) Choice E is correct

A. $\frac{3}{2} \times \frac{5}{9} = \frac{5}{6}$ is not a whole number

B. $\frac{1}{3} + \frac{1}{4} = \frac{4+3}{12} = \frac{7}{12}$ is not a whole number

C. $\frac{40}{6} = \frac{20}{3} = 6.66$ is not a whole number

D. $3.5 + 2 = 5.5$ is not a whole number

E. $3.5 + \frac{4}{8} = 3.5 + 0.5 = 4$ is a whole number

4) Choice D is correct

8 cubed is: $8 \times 8 \times 8 = 64 \times 8 = 512$

5) Choice A is correct

Let x be the number, then; $\frac{2}{3}x = 16 \rightarrow x = \frac{3 \times 16}{2} = 24$, Therefore: $\frac{5}{3}x = \frac{5}{3} \times 24 = 40$

6) Choice D is correct

Use formula of rectangle prism volume. $V = (length)(width)(height) \Rightarrow 3{,}000 = (30)(10)(height). \Rightarrow height = 3{,}000 \div 300 = 10$ feet

7) Choice D is correct

Number of boxes equal to: $\frac{450}{25} = \frac{90}{5} = 18$

8) Choice D is correct

The angle x and 60 are complementary angles. Therefore: $x + 60 = 180, 180° - 60° = 120°$

9) Choice E is correct

Use simple interest formula: $I = prt$ (I = interest, p = principal, r = rate, t = time)

$I = (13{,}500)(0.045)(2) = \$1{,}215$

10) Choice C is correct

$\frac{504}{600} = 0.84 = 84\%$. 504 is 84% of 600. Therefore, the discount is: $100\% - 84\% = 16\%$

11) Choice D is correct

Use distance formula: $Distance = Rate \times time \Rightarrow 527 = 62 \times T$, divide both sides by 62.

$\frac{527}{62} = T \Rightarrow T = 8.5\ hours.$ Change hours to minutes for the decimal part.

$0.5\ hours = 0.5 \times 60 = 30\ minutes$

12) Choice C is correct

The rate of construction company $= \frac{40\ cm}{1\ min} = 40\frac{cm}{min}$

Height of the wall after 50 $min = \frac{40\ cm}{1\ min} \times 50\ min = 2{,}000cm$

Let x be the height of wall, then $\frac{2}{3}x = 2{,}000\ cm \rightarrow x = \frac{3 \times 2{,}000}{2} \rightarrow x = 3{,}000\ cm = 30m$

13) Choice C is correct

Let's review the choices provided:

A. $28 - 2 = 26 \rightarrow \frac{26}{2} = 13 \neq 3$

B. $28 - 5 = 23 \rightarrow \frac{23}{5} = 4.6 \neq 3$

C. $28 - 7 = 21 \rightarrow \frac{21}{7} = 3 = 3$

D. $28 - 12 = 16 \rightarrow \frac{16}{12} = 1.33 \neq 3$

E. $28 - 28 = 0 \rightarrow \frac{0}{28} = 0 \neq 3$

14) Choice C is correct

Speed of car A is: $\frac{700}{7} = 100$ miles per hour , Speed of car B is: $\frac{700}{5} = 140$ miles per hour

$\rightarrow 140 - 100 = 40$ miles per hour

15) Choice C is correct

x is the number of all sales profit and 4% of it is: $4\% \times x = 0.04x$, Employee's revenue: $0.04x + 8000$

16) Choice B is correct

$\frac{1}{5} \cong 0.2$ $\frac{5}{3} \cong 1.66$ $\frac{8}{11} \cong 0.73$ $\frac{2}{3} = 0.66$

$$\frac{5}{3} > \frac{8}{11} > \frac{2}{3} > \frac{1}{5}$$

17) Choice D is correct

The ratio of boys to girls is 3: 2. Therefore, there are 3 boys out of 5 students. To find the answer, first divide the total number of students by 5, then multiply the result by 3.

$700 \div 5 = 140 \Rightarrow 140 \times 3 = 420$

18) Choice E is correct

$\frac{(8+6)^2}{2} + 6 = \frac{(14)^2}{2} + 6 = \frac{196}{2} + 6 = 98 + 6 = 104$

19) Choice D is correct

$y = 5ab + 2b^4$, Plug in the values of a and b in the equation: $a = 3$ and $b = 2$

$y = 5(3)(2) + 2(2)^4 = 30 + 2(16) = 30 + 32 = 62$

20) Choice B is correct

Use the formula of the area of circles. $Area = \pi r^2 \Rightarrow 49\pi = \pi r^2 \Rightarrow 49 = r^2 \Rightarrow r = 7$

Radius of the circle is 7. Now, use the circumference formula: Circumference $= 2\pi r = 2\pi(7) = 14\pi$

21) Choice D is correct

$0.8x = (0.4) \times 20 \rightarrow x = 10 \rightarrow (x+7)^2 = (10+7)^2 = (17)^2 = 289$

22) Choice D is correct

Prime factorizing of $18 = 2 \times 3 \times 3$, Prime factorizing of $24 = 2 \times 2 \times 2 \times 3$

$\text{GCF} = 2 \times 3 = 6$

23) Choice A is correct

The sum of all angles in a quadrilateral is 360 degrees. Let x be the smallest angle in the quadrilateral. Then the angles are: $x, 2x, 3x, 4x$,

$x + 2x + 3x + 4x = 360 \rightarrow 10x = 360 \rightarrow x = 36$, The angles in the quadrilateral are: $36°, 72°, 108°$, and $144°$, The smallest angle is 36 degrees.

24) Choice E is correct

Length of the rectangle is: $\frac{4}{5} \times 30 = 24$, Perimeter of rectangle is: $2 \times (24 + 30) = 108$

25) Choice A is correct

$\frac{3}{4}$ of $160 = \frac{3}{4} \times 160 = 120$, $\frac{2}{3}$ of $120 = \frac{2}{3} \times 120 = 80$

SSAT Upper Level Mathematics Practice Test 3 Section 1

1) Choice A is correct

Number of rotates in 12 second equals to: $\frac{200 \times 12}{8} = 300$

2) Choice D is correct

Number of packs equal to: $\frac{23}{3} \cong 7.666$, Therefore, the school must purchase 8 packs.

3) Choice D is correct

$\frac{25}{A} + 1 = 6 \rightarrow \frac{25}{A} = 6 - 1 = 5, \rightarrow 25 = 5A \rightarrow A = \frac{25}{5} = 5, 30 + A = 30 + 5 = 35$

4) Choice C is correct

The area of the floor is: $7\ cm \times 24\ cm = 168\ cm^2$, The number of tiles needed =

$$168 \div 8 = 21$$

5) Choice D is correct

A. Number of books sold in April is: 560

Number of books sold in July is: $850 \rightarrow \frac{560}{850} = \frac{56}{85} \cong 0.66$

B. number of books sold in July is: 850

Half the number of books sold in May is: $\frac{1{,}240}{2} = 620 \rightarrow 850 > 620$

C. number of books sold in June is: 290

Half the number of books sold in April is: $\frac{560}{2} = 280 \rightarrow 290 \neq 280$

D. $560 + 290 = 850 = 850$

E. $560 < 850$

6) Choice D is correct

$$12.124 \div 0.004 = \frac{\frac{12{,}124}{1{,}000}}{\frac{4}{1{,}000}} = \frac{12{,}124}{4} = 3{,}031$$

7) Choice E is correct

The digit in tens place is 7.The digit in the thousandths place is 4. Therefore; $7 + 4 = 11$

8) Choice A is correct

First, find the number. Let x be the number. Write the equation and solve for x. 150% of a number is 75, then: $1.5 \times x = 75 \rightarrow x = 75 \div 1.5 = 50$, 80% of 50 is: $0.8 \times 50 = 40$

9) Choice E is correct

Amy earns $\$30.00$ *per hour* now. $\$30.00$ *per hour* is 20 percent more than her previous rate. Let x be her rate before her raise. Then: $x + 0.20x = 30 \rightarrow 1.2x = 30 \rightarrow x = \frac{30}{1.2} = 25$

John earns $\$28.80$ *per hour* now. $\$28.80$ *per hour* is 20 percent more than his previous rate. Let x be John's rate before his raise. Then: $x + 0.20x = 28.80 \rightarrow 1.2x = 28.80 \rightarrow x = \frac{28.80}{1.2} = 24$, Amy earned $\$1.00$ more per hour than John before their raises

10) Choice A is correct

$$\frac{1\frac{3}{4}+\frac{1}{3}}{2\frac{1}{2}-\frac{15}{8}} = \frac{\frac{7}{4}+\frac{1}{3}}{\frac{5}{2}-\frac{15}{8}} = \frac{\frac{21+4}{12}}{\frac{20-15}{8}} = \frac{\frac{25}{12}}{\frac{5}{8}} = \frac{25 \times 8}{12 \times 5} = \frac{5 \times 2}{3 \times 1} = \frac{10}{3} \cong 3.33$$

11) Choice B is correct

$2 \leq x < 4 \rightarrow$ Multiply all sides of the inequality by 2. Then: $2 \times 2 \leq 2 \times x < 2 \times 4 \rightarrow 4 \leq 2x < 8$, All 1 to all sides. Then: $\rightarrow 4 + 1 \leq 2x + 1 < 8 + 1 \rightarrow 5 \leq 2x + 1 < 9$

Minimum value of $2x + 1$ is 5.

12) Choice B is correct

$6 \blacksquare 13 = \sqrt{6^2 + 13} = \sqrt{36 + 13} = \sqrt{49} = 7$

13) Choice B is correct

$Average = \frac{sum\ of\ terms}{number\ of\ terms}$, The sum of the weight of all girls is: $18 \times 55 = 990\ kg$

The sum of the weight of all boys is: $32 \times 62 = 1{,}984\ kg$, The sum of the weight of all students is: $990 + 1{,}984 = 2{,}974 kg$, The average weight of the 50 students: $Average = \frac{2{,}974}{50} = 59.48\ kg$

14) Choice A is correct

Let x be the capacity of one tank. Then, $\frac{2}{5}x = 250 \rightarrow x = \frac{250 \times 5}{2} = 625$ Liters

The amount of water in three tanks is equal to: $3 \times 625 = 1{,}875$ Liters

15) Choice D is correct

$$8.5 \div 0.17 = \frac{8.5}{0.17} = \frac{\frac{85}{10}}{\frac{17}{100}} = \frac{85 \times 100}{17 \times 10} = \frac{85}{17} \times \frac{100}{10} = 5 \times 10 = 50$$

16) Choice A is correct

Let x be the cost of one-kilogram orange, then: $2x + (2 \times 4.2) = 26.4 \rightarrow 2x + 8.4 = 26.4 \rightarrow 2x = 26.4 - 8.4 \rightarrow 2x = 18 \rightarrow x = \frac{18}{2} = \$9$

17) Choice A is correct

$$x = 35 + 125 = 160$$

18) Choice C is correct

Let's write equations based on the information provided:

$Michelle = Karen - 9, Michelle = David - 4, Karen + Michelle + David = 82$

$Karen - 9 = Michelle \Rightarrow Karen = Michelle + 9$

$Karen + Michelle + David = 82$

Now, replace the ages of Karen and David by Michelle. Then:

$Michelle + 9 + Michelle + Michelle + 4 = 82$

$3 \times Michelle + 13 = 82 \Rightarrow 3 \times Michelle = 82 - 13$

$3 \times Michelle = 69 , Michelle = 23$

19) Choice B is correct

Let b be the amount of time Alec can do the job, then,

$\frac{1}{a} + \frac{1}{b} = \frac{1}{50} \rightarrow \frac{1}{300} + \frac{1}{b} = \frac{1}{50} \rightarrow \frac{1}{b} = \frac{1}{50} - \frac{1}{300} = \frac{5}{300} = \frac{1}{60}$, Then: $b = 60$ minutes

20) Choice C is correct

The smallest number is -15. To find the largest possible value of one of the other five integers, we need to choose the smallest possible integers for four of them. Let x be the largest number. Then: $-72 = (-15) + (-14) + (-13) + (-12) + (-11) + x \rightarrow -72 = -65 + x, \rightarrow x = -72 + 65 = -7$

21) Choice B is correct

The equation of a line in slope intercept form is: $y = mx + b$. Solve for y. $4x - 2y = 14 \Rightarrow -2y = 14 - 4x \Rightarrow y = (14 - 4x) \div (-2) \Rightarrow y = 2x - 7$

The slope is 2. The slope of the line perpendicular to this line is: $m_1 \times m_2 = -1 \Rightarrow 2 \times m_2 = -1 \Rightarrow m_2 = -\frac{1}{2}$

22) Choice C is correct

Use simple interest formula: $I = prt$ (I = interest, p = principal, r = rate, t = time)

$I = (7{,}000)(0.055)(5) = \$1{,}925$

23) Choice D is correct

The amount of money for x bookshelf is: $100x$, Then, the total cost of all bookshelves is equal to:$100x + 900$, The total cost, in dollar, per bookshelf is: $\frac{\text{Total cost}}{\text{number of items}} = \frac{100x+900}{x}$

24) Choice B is correct

Choices A, C and D are incorrect because 60% of each of the numbers is non-whole number.

A. 49, 60% of $49 = 0.60 \times 49 = 29.4$
B. 35, 60% of $35 = 0.60 \times 35 = 21$
C. 32, 60% of $32 = 0.60 \times 32 = 19.2$
D. 16, 60% of $16 = 0.60 \times 16 = 9.6$
E. 12, 60% of $12 = 0.60 \times 12 = 7.2$

25) Choice E is correct

If the length of the box is 36 , then the width of the box is one third of it, 12, and the height of the box is 4 (one third of the width). The volume of the box is:

$V = (length)(width)(height) = (36)(12)(4) = 1{,}728\ cm^3$

SSAT Upper Level Mathematics Practice Test 3 Section 2

1) Choice C is correct

$\frac{19+11}{2} = \frac{30}{2} = 15$ Then, $15 - 11 = 4$

2) Choice D is correct

Let's review the choices provided:

A. $x = 2 \rightarrow$ The perimeter of the figure is: $2 + 4 + 2 + 2 + 2 = 12 \neq 26$
B. $x = 3 \rightarrow$ The perimeter of the figure is: $2 + 4 + 2 + 3 + 3 = 14 \neq 26$
C. $x = 6 \rightarrow$ The perimeter of the figure is: $2 + 4 + 2 + 6 + 6 = 20 \neq 26$
D. $x = 9 \rightarrow$ The perimeter of the figure is: $2 + 4 + 2 + 9 + 9 = 26 = 26$
E. $x = 12 \rightarrow$ The perimeter of the figure is: $2 + 4 + 2 + 12 + 12 = 32 \neq 26$

3) Choice C is correct

$\frac{92{,}501}{305} \cong 303.2819 \cong 303$

4) Choice E is correct

Alex's mark is k less than Jason's mark. Then, from the choices provided Alex's mark can only be $15 - k$.

5) Choice A is correct

The Area that one liter of paint is required: $62cm \times 100cm = 6{,}200cm^2$

Remember: $1\ m^2 = 10{,}000\ cm^2\ (100 \times 100 = 10{,}000), then, 6{,}200cm^2 = 0.62\ m^2$

Number of liters of paint we need: $\frac{62}{0.62} = 100$ liters

6) Choice C is correct

Let x be the original price. If the price of the sofa is decreased by 25% to \$432, then:
$75\ \%\ of\ x = 432 \Rightarrow 0.75x = 432 \Rightarrow x = 432 \div 0.75 = 576$

7) Choice B is correct

$750 - 8\frac{7}{15} = (749 - 8) + \left(\frac{15}{15} - \frac{7}{15}\right) = 741\frac{8}{15}$

8) Choice E is correct

Number of times that the driver rests $= \frac{15}{3} = 5$, Driver's rest time $= 1\ hour\ and\ 12\ minutes = 72\ minutes$, Then, 5×72 minutes $= 360$ minutes, $1\ hour = 60\ minutes \rightarrow 360\ minutes = 6\ hours$

9) Choice E is correct

Let's review the options provided:

A. $8 \times \frac{1}{2} = \frac{8}{2} = 4 = 4$
B. $20 \times \frac{1}{5} = \frac{20}{5} = 4 = 4$
C. $2 \times \frac{4}{2} = \frac{8}{2} = 4 = 4$
D. $4 \times \frac{5}{5} = \frac{20}{5} = 4 = 4$
E. $4 \times \frac{1}{4} = \frac{4}{4} = 1 \neq 4$

10) Choice A is correct

Find the difference of each pairs of numbers: $2, 3, 5, 8, 12, 17,$ ___, 30

The difference of 2 and 3 is 1, 3 and 5 is 2, 5 and 8 is 3, 8 and 12 is 4, 12 and 17 is 5, 17 and next number should be 6. The number is $17 + 6 = 23$

11) Choice B is correct

Number of Mathematics book: $0.3 \times 800 = 240$, Number of English books: $0.15 \times 800 = 120$,Product of number of Mathematics and number of English books: $240 \times 120 = 28{,}800$

12) Choice D is correct

The angle α is: $0.3 \times 360 = 108°$, The angle β is: $0.15 \times 360 = 54°$

13) Choice E is correct

The length of the rectangle is 24. Then, its width is 8. $24 \div 3 = 8$

$$Perimeter\ of\ a\ rectangle = 2 \times width + 2 \times length = 2 \times 8 + 2 \times 24 = 16 + 48 = 64$$

14) Choice E is correct

$3y + 2 < 29 \rightarrow 3y < 29 - 2 \rightarrow 3y < 27 \rightarrow y < 9$, The only choice that is less than 9 is E.

15) Choice D is correct

The capacity of a red box is 20% bigger than the capacity of a blue box and it can hold 36 books. Therefore, we want to find a number that 20% bigger than that number is 36. Let x be that number. Then: $1.20 \times x = 36$, Divide both sides of the equation by 1.2. Then:

$$x = \frac{36}{1.20} = 30$$

16) Choice B is correct

First, simplify inside the parenthesis: $8 + (A \times 12) = 28 \rightarrow 8 + 12A = 28$

Subtract 8 from both sides: $8 + 12A - 8 = 28 - 8 \rightarrow 12A = 20$

Divide both sides by 12: $12A = 20 \rightarrow \frac{12A}{12} = \frac{20}{12}$. Now, simplify the fraction: $A = \frac{20}{12} = \frac{5}{3}$

17) Choice D is correct

Amount of available petrol in tank: $60.2 - 5.28 - 25.9 + 10.31 = 39.33$ liters

18) Choice E is correct

We have two equations and three unknown variables, therefore x cannot be obtained.

19) Choice C is correct

$96 = 8x \times 4 \rightarrow x = 96 \div 4 = 24 \rightarrow x = 3$

x equals to 3. Let's review the choices provided:

A. $x + 4 \rightarrow 3 + 4 = 7$ 96 is not divisible by 7.
B. $2x - 1 \rightarrow 2 \times 3 - 1 = 5$ 96 is not divisible by 5.
C. $5x - 3 \rightarrow 5 \times 3 - 3 = 12$ 96 is divisible by 12.
D. $x \times 3 \rightarrow 3 \times 3 = 9$ 96 is not divisible by 9.
E. $3x + 1 \rightarrow 3 \times 3 + 1 = 10$ 96 is not divisible by 10.

The answer is C

20) Choice A is correct

Perimeter of figure A is: $2\pi r = 2\pi \frac{16}{2} = 16\pi = 16 \times 3 = 48$, Area of figure B is: $4 \times 13 = 52$,
$Average = \frac{48+52}{2} = \frac{100}{2} = 50$

21) Choice B is correct

The angles on a straight line add up to 180 degrees. Then: $x + 22 + y + 2x + y = 180$, Then,
$3x + 2y = 180 - 22 \rightarrow 3(28) + 2y = 158 \rightarrow 2y = 158 - 84 = 74 \rightarrow y = 37$

22) Choice D is correct

$\frac{1}{6}$ of 40 is 6.66. Let's review the choices provided:

A. $0.3 \times 6 = 1.8$
B. $0.3 \times 5 = 1.5$
C. $0.2 \times 30 = 6$
D. $0.2 \times 35 = 7$
E. $0.2 \times 39.5 = 7.9$

Option D is the closest to 6.66

23) Choice C is correct

Set of numbers that are not composite between 1 and 18: $A = \{2, 3, 5, 7, 11, 13, 17\}$

$$Probability = \frac{number\ of\ desired\ outcomes}{number\ of\ total\ outcomes} = \frac{7}{18}$$

24) Choice C is correct

$$812 \div 3 = \frac{812}{3} = \frac{800 + 10 + 2}{3} = \frac{800}{3} + \frac{10}{3} + \frac{2}{3}$$

25) Choice D is correct

$$\frac{2}{5} \times 35 = \frac{70}{5} = 14$$

SSAT Upper Level Mathematics Practice Test 4 Section 1

1) Choice C is correct

$0.03 \times 12.00 = \frac{3}{100} \times \frac{12}{1} = \frac{36}{100} = 0.36$

2) Choice E is correct

$x - 10 = -10 \rightarrow x = -10 + 10 \rightarrow x = 0$, Then; $x \times 3 = 0 \times 3 = 0$

3) Choice B is correct

Digit 4 is in the tenths place.

4) Choice D is correct

Number of packs needed equals to: $\frac{16}{3} \cong 5.33$, Then Mia must purchase 6 packs.

5) Choice D is correct

15 minutes $= 0.25$ hour. So, his average speed was: $\frac{1.25}{0.25} = 5$ miles per hour

6) Choice D is correct

The amount of flour is: $x - 55$

7) Choice B is correct

The time it takes to drive from city A to city B is: $\frac{2{,}600}{68} = 38.23$, It's approximately 38 hours.

8) Choice B is correct

The perimeter of the quadrilateral is: $6 + 20 + 9 + 31 = 66$

9) Choice C is correct

Number of males in the classroom is: $60 - 42 = 18$

Then, the percentage of males in the classroom is: $\frac{18}{60} \times 100 = 0.3 \times 100 = 30\%$

10) Choice D is correct

Let x be the fourth quarter rate, then: $\frac{92+88+86+x}{4} = 90$, Multiply both sides of the above equation by 4. Then: $4 \times \left(\frac{92+88+86+x}{4}\right) = 4 \times 90 \rightarrow 92 + 88 + 86 + x = 360 \rightarrow 266 + x - 360 \rightarrow x = 360 - 266 = 94$

11) Choice C is correct

Let x be the number. Write the equation and solve for x. $\frac{2}{3} \times 18 = \frac{2}{5}x \rightarrow \frac{2\times18}{3} = \frac{2x}{5}$, use cross multiplication to solve for x. $5 \times 36 = 2x \times 3 \Rightarrow 180 = 6x \Rightarrow x = 30$

12) Choice A is correct

For one person the total cost is: $\$8.25$, Therefore, for four persons, the total cost is: $4 \times \$8.25 = \$33$

13) Choice C is correct

Three times of $24{,}000$ is $72{,}000$. One sixth of them cancelled their tickets. One sixth of $72{,}000$ equals $12{,}000$ ($\frac{1}{6} \times 72{,}000 = 12{,}000$). $60{,}000$ ($72{,}000 - 12{,}000 = 60{,}000$) fans are attending this week.

14) Choice A is correct

The equation of a line in slope intercept form is: $y = mx + b$. Solve for y. $7x + y = 12 \Rightarrow y = -7x + 12$, $y = -7x + 12$. The slope of this line is -7.The slope of the line perpendicular to this line is: $m_1 \times m_2 = -1 \Rightarrow -7 \times m_2 = -1 \Rightarrow m_2 = \frac{1}{7}$

15) Choice C is correct

Use the information provided in the question to draw the shape.

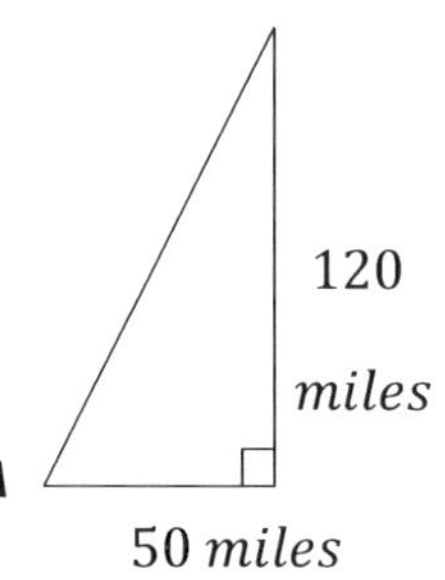

Use Pythagorean Theorem: $a^2 + b^2 = c^2$

$50^2 + 120^2 = c^2 \Rightarrow 2{,}500 + 14{,}400 = c^2 \Rightarrow 16{,}900 = c^2 \Rightarrow c = 130$ miles

16) Choice A is correct

Let x be the number of years. Therefore, $\$2{,}000$ per year equals $2000x$. Starting from $\$24{,}000$ annual salary means you should add that amount to $2000x$. Income more than that is: $I > 2{,}000\,x + 24{,}000$

17) Choice D is correct

Ratio of women to men in city A: $\frac{816}{850} = 0.96$

Ratio of women to men in city B: $\frac{456}{480} = 0.95$

Ratio of women to men in city C: $\frac{266}{290} = 0.91$

Ratio of women to men in city D: $\frac{539}{550} = 0.98$

0.98 is the maximum ratio of woman to man in the four cities.

18) Choice D is correct

Percentage of men in city $= \frac{850}{1{,}666} \times 100 = 51.02\%$, Percentage of women in city $C = \frac{266}{556} \times 100 = 47.84\%$, Percentage of men in city A to percentage of women in city $C = \frac{51.02}{47.84} \cong 1.07$

19) Choice B is correct

Let the number of women should be added to city D be x, then:

$$\frac{539 + x}{550} = 1.4 \rightarrow 539 + x = 550 \times 1.4 = 770 \rightarrow x = 231$$

20) Choice A is correct

The length of MN is equal to: $3x + 5x = 8x$, Then: $8x = 40 \rightarrow x = \frac{40}{8} = 5$

The length of ON is equal to: $5x = 5 \times 5 = 25\ cm$

21) Choice A is correct

$$\frac{x}{2+3} = \frac{y}{10-7} \rightarrow \frac{x}{5} = \frac{y}{3} \rightarrow 5y = 3x \rightarrow y = \frac{3}{5}x$$

22) Choice A is correct

$$\sqrt[5]{x^{16}} = \sqrt[5]{x^{15} \times x} = \sqrt[5]{x^{15}} \times \sqrt[5]{x} = x^{\frac{15}{5}} \times \sqrt[5]{x} = x^3\sqrt[5]{x}$$

23) Choice C is correct

The average speed of John is: $150 \div 6 = 25\ km$, The average speed of Alice is: $180 \div 4 = 45\ km$. Write the ratio and simplify. $25 : 45 \Rightarrow 5 : 9$

24) Choice D is correct

Smallest 4–digit number is 1,000, and biggest 4–digit number is 9,999. The difference is: 8,999

25) Choice D is correct

Perimeter of rectangle A is equal to: $2 \times (8 + 4) = 2 \times 12 = 24$, Perimeter of rectangle B is equal to: $2 \times (5 + 4) = 2 \times 9 = 18$, Therefore: $\frac{18}{24} \times 100 = 0.75 \times 100 = 75\%$

SSAT Upper Level Mathematics Practice Test 4 Section 2

1) Choice C is correct

$5\frac{3}{7} \times 4\frac{1}{5} = \frac{38}{7} \times \frac{21}{5} = \frac{38 \times 21}{7 \times 5} = \frac{798}{35} = \frac{114}{5} = 22\frac{4}{5}$

2) Choice E is correct

A. $\frac{2}{3} \times \frac{9}{5} = \frac{6}{5}$ is not a whole number

B. $\frac{1}{2} + \frac{1}{4} = \frac{2+1}{4} = \frac{3}{4}$ is not a whole number

C. $\frac{21}{6} = \frac{7}{2} = 3.5$ is not a whole number

D. $2.5 + 1 = 3.5$ is not a whole number

E. $2.5 + \frac{7}{2} = 2.5 + 3.5 = 6$ is a whole number

3) Choice A is correct

$0.42 \times 11.8 = \frac{42}{100} \times \frac{118}{10} = \frac{42 \times 118}{100 \times 10} = \frac{4956}{1000} = 4.956$

4) Choice B is correct

$\frac{530.40}{624} = 0.85 = 85\%$, 530.40 is 85% of 624. Therefore, the discount is:

$$100\% - 85\% = 15\%$$

5) Choice E is correct

Let x be the number, then; $\frac{2}{5}x = 12 \rightarrow x = \frac{5 \times 12}{2} = 30$, Therefore: $\frac{2}{3}x = \frac{2}{3} \times 30 = 20$

6) Choice C is correct

Use distance formula: $Distance = Rate \times time \Rightarrow 420 = 50 \times T$, divide both sides by $50. 420 \div 50 = T \Rightarrow T = 8.4\, hours$. Change hours to minutes for the decimal part. $0.4\, hours = 0.4 \times 60 = 24\, minutes$

7) Choice E is correct

Use formula of rectangle prism volume. $V = (length)(width)(height) \Rightarrow 2{,}000 = (25)(10)(height) \Rightarrow height = 2{,}000 \div 250 = 8\, feet$

8) Choice B is correct

Use simple interest formula: $I = prt$ ($I =$ interest, $p =$ principal, $r =$ rate, $t =$ time)

$I = (12{,}000)(0.035)(2) = \$840$

9) Choice E is correct

The angle x and 35 are supplementary angles. Therefore: $x + 35 = 180$, $180° - 35° = 145°$

10) Choice E is correct

Number of boxes equal to: $\frac{408}{24} = \frac{102}{6} = \frac{34}{2} = 17$

11) Choice C is correct

The rate of construction company $= \frac{30\ cm}{1\ min} = 30\ \frac{cm}{min}$, Height of the wall after $40\ min = \frac{30\ cm}{1\ min} \times 40\ min = 1{,}200\ cm$, Let x be the height of wall, then $\frac{3}{4}x = 1{,}200\ cm \rightarrow x = \frac{4 \times 1{,}200}{3} \rightarrow x = 1{,}600\ cm = 16\ m$

12) Choice D is correct

7 cubed is: $7 \times 7 \times 7 = 49 \times 7 = 343$

13) Choice C is correct

Let's review the choices provided:

A. $24 - 2 = 22 \rightarrow \frac{22}{2} = 11 \neq 3$

B. $24 - 4 = 20 \rightarrow \frac{20}{4} = 5 \neq 3$

C. $24 - 6 = 18 \rightarrow \frac{18}{6} = 3 = 3$

D. $24 - 12 = 12 \rightarrow \frac{12}{12} = 1 \neq 3$

E. $24 - 24 = 0 \rightarrow \frac{0}{24} = 0 \neq 3$

14) Choice E is correct

Speed of car A is: $\frac{600}{8} = 75$ miles per hour, Speed of car B is: $\frac{600}{7.5} = 80$ miles per hour, $\rightarrow 80 - 75 = 5$ miles per hour

15) Choice E is correct

The ratio of boys to girls is 2: 3. Therefore, there are 2 boys out of 5 students. To find the answer, first divide the total number of students by 5, then multiply the result by 2.

$600 \div 5 = 120 \Rightarrow 120 \times 2 = 240$

16) Choice A is correct

$$\frac{(7+5)^2}{4} + 5 = \frac{(12)^2}{4} + 5 = \frac{144}{4} + 5 = 36 + 5 = 41$$

17) Choice E is correct

$y = 4ab + 3b^3$, Plug in the values of a and b in the equation: $a = 2\ and\ b = 3$

$y = 4\,(2)\,(3) + 3\,(3)^3 = 24 + 3(27) = 24 + 81 = 105$

18) Choice C is correct

x is the number of all sales profit and 2% of it is: $2\% \times x = 0.02x$, Employee's revenue: $0.02x + 7{,}000$

19) Choice A is correct

$\frac{2}{3} \cong 0.67$ $\frac{5}{7} \cong 0.71$ $\frac{8}{11} \cong 0.73$ $\frac{3}{4} = 0.75$

$$\frac{2}{3} < \frac{5}{7} < \frac{8}{11} < \frac{3}{4}$$

20) Choice C is correct

Use the formula of the area of circles. $Area = \pi r^2 \Rightarrow 64\pi = \pi r^2 \Rightarrow 64 = r^2 \Rightarrow r = 8$

Radius of the circle is 8. Now, use the circumference formula:

Circumference $= 2\pi r = 2\pi\,(8) = 16\,\pi$

21) Choice D is correct

$0.6x = (0.3) \times 20 \rightarrow x = 10 \rightarrow (x+5)^2 = (10+5)^2 = (15)^2 = 225$

22) Choice C is correct

Prime factorizing of $36 = 2 \times 2 \times 3 \times 3$, Prime factorizing of $54 = 2 \times 3 \times 3 \times 3$

$GCF = 2 \times 3 \times 3 = 18$

23) Choice C is correct

Length of the rectangle is: $\frac{5}{4} \times 16 = 20$, Perimeter of rectangle is: $2 \times (20 + 16) = 72$

24) Choice B is correct

$\frac{2}{5}$ Of $120 = \frac{2}{5} \times 120 = 48$, $\frac{1}{4}$ Of $48 = \frac{1}{4} \times 48 = 12$

25) Choice B is correct

The sum of all angles in a quadrilateral is 360 degrees. Let x be the smallest angle in the quadrilateral. Then the angles are: $x, 4x, 6x, 7x$, $x + 4x + 6x + 7x = 360 \rightarrow 18x = 360 \rightarrow x = 20$, The angles in the quadrilateral are: $20°, 80°, 120°$, and $140°$

SSAT Upper Level Mathematics Practice Test 5 Section 1

1) Choice B is correct

1,000 times the number is 40.5. Let x be the number, then: $1{,}000x = 40.5, x = \frac{40.5}{1{,}000} = 0.0405$

2) Choice E is correct

In the question, there are two equations and three variables. Therefore, it cannot be determined from the information given.

3) Choice D is correct

x and z are colinear. y and $5x$ are colinear. Therefore,

$x + z = y + 5x, subtract\ x\ from\ both\ sides, then, z = y + 4x$. Only choice D is correct. All other choices are wrong.

4) Choice D is correct

Check each choice.

A. $\frac{3}{4} > 0.8$ $\quad\frac{3}{4} = 0.75$ and it is less than 0.8. Not true!
B. $10\% = \frac{2}{5}$ $\quad 10\% = \frac{1}{10} < \frac{2}{5}$. Not True!
C. $3 < \frac{5}{2}$ $\quad\frac{5}{2} = 2.5 < 3$. Not True!
D. $\frac{5}{6} > 0.8$ $\quad\frac{5}{6} = 0.8333\ldots$ and it is greater than 0.8. Bingo!
E. None of them above $\quad$ Not True!

5) Choice C is correct

40% of 60 equals to: $0.40 \times 60 = 24$. 12% of 600 equals to: $0.12 \times 600 = 72$

40% of 60 is added to 12% of 600: $24 + 72 = 96$

6) Choice E is correct

The digit in tens place is 1. The digit in the thousandths place is 4. Therefore; $1 + 4 = 5$

7) Choice E is correct

The amount of money that Jack earns for one hour: $\frac{\$616}{44} = \$14$, Number of additional hours that he need to work in order to make enough money is: $\frac{\$826-\$616}{1.5\times\$14} = 10$

Number of total hours is: $44 + 10 = 54$

8) Choice D is correct

$$12.124 \div 0.002 = \frac{\frac{12,124}{1,000}}{\frac{2}{1,000}} = \frac{12,124}{2} = 6,062$$

9) Choice A is correct

$$\frac{1\frac{5}{4}+\frac{1}{3}}{2\frac{1}{2}-\frac{15}{8}} = \frac{\frac{9}{4}+\frac{1}{3}}{\frac{5}{2}-\frac{15}{8}} = \frac{\frac{27+4}{12}}{\frac{20-15}{8}} = \frac{\frac{31}{12}}{\frac{5}{8}} = \frac{31 \times 8}{12 \times 5} = \frac{31 \times 2}{3 \times 5} = \frac{62}{15} \cong 4.133$$

10) Choice A is correct

First, find the number. Let x be the number. Write the equation and solve for x. 150% of a number is 75, then:$1.5 \times x = 75 \rightarrow x = 75 \div 1.5 = 50$, 90% of 50 is: $0.9 \times 50 = 45$

11) Choice E is correct.

$$y = (-3x^3)^2 = (-3)^2(x^3)^2 = 9x^6$$

12) Choice A is correct

Let x be the capacity of one tank. Then, $\frac{2}{5}x = 200 \rightarrow x = \frac{200 \times 5}{2} = 500$ Liters

The amount of water in three tanks is equal to: $3 \times 500 = 1,500$ Liters

13) Choice D is correct

Let q be the quotient of 7.5 and 0.15 then: $q = \frac{7.5}{0.15} = \frac{\frac{75}{10}}{\frac{15}{100}} = \frac{75 \times 100}{15 \times 10} = \frac{75}{15} \times \frac{100}{10} = 5 \times 10 = 50$

14) Choice B is correct

$Average = \frac{sum\ of\ terms}{number\ of\ terms}$, The sum of the weight of all girls is: $18 \times 60 = 1,080\ kg$

The sum of the weight of all boys is: $32 \times 62 = 1,984\ kg$, The sum of the weight of all students is: $1,080 + 1,984 = 3,064\ kg$, $Average = \frac{3,064}{50} = 61.28\ kg$

15) Choice C is correct

$1 \leq x < 4 \rightarrow 2 \times 1 \leq 2 \times x < 2 \times 4 \rightarrow 2 \leq 2x < 8, \rightarrow 2 + 1 \leq 2x + 1 < 8 + 1 \rightarrow 3 \leq 2x + 1 < 9$, Minimum value of $2x + 1$ is 3.

16) Choice B is correct

$x = 20 + 125 = 145$

17) Choice B is correct

Let b be the amount of time Alec can do the job, then,

$\frac{1}{a}+\frac{1}{b}=\frac{1}{100} \rightarrow \frac{1}{300}+\frac{1}{b}=\frac{1}{100} \rightarrow \frac{1}{b}=\frac{1}{100}-\frac{1}{300}=\frac{2}{300}=\frac{1}{150}$, Then: $b = 150$ minutes

18) Choice C is correct

The smallest number is -15. To find the largest possible value of one of the other five integers, we need to choose the smallest possible integers for four of them. Let x be the largest number. Then: $-70 = (-15) + (-14) + (-13) + (-12) + (-11) + x \rightarrow -70 = -65 + x, \rightarrow x = -70 + 65 = -5$

19) Choice B is correct

Let's review the options provided.

A. 4. In 4 years, David will be 46 and Ava will be 10. 46 is not 4 times 10.
B. 6. In 6 years, David will be 48 and Ava will be 12. 48 is 4 times 12!
C. 8. In 8 years, David will be 50 and Ava will be 14. 50 is not 4 times 14.
D. 10. In 10 years, David will be 52 and Ava will be 16. 52 is not 4 times 16.
E. 14. In 14 years, David will be 56 and Ava will be 20. 56 is not 4 times 20.

20) Choice A is correct

Let x be the integer. Then: $2x - 5 = 73$, Add 5 both sides: $2x = 78$, Divide both sides by 2:

$$x = 39$$

21) Choice A is correct

The equation of a line in slope intercept form is: $y = mx + b$. Solve for y.

$$x - 2y = 12 \Rightarrow -2y = 12 - x \Rightarrow y = (12 - x) \div (-2) \Rightarrow y = \frac{1}{2}x - 6$$

The slope is $\frac{1}{2}$. The slope of the line perpendicular to this line is:

$$m_1 \times m^2 = -1 \Rightarrow \frac{1}{2} \times m^2 = -1 \Rightarrow m^2 = -2$$

22) Choice D is correct

Use the information provided in the question to draw the shape.

150 *miles*

Use Pythagorean Theorem: $a^2 + b^2 = c^2$

$80^2 + 150^2 = c^2 \Rightarrow 6{,}400 + 22{,}500 = c^2 \Rightarrow 28{,}900 = c^2 \Rightarrow c = 170$ miles

Port A

80 *miles*

23) Choice B is correct

Choices A, C, D and E are incorrect because 80% of each of the numbers is non-whole number.

A. 49, $\quad$ 80% of 49 $= 0.80 \times 49 = 39.2$
B. 35, $\quad$ 80% of 35 $= 0.80 \times 35 = 28$

C. 32, 80% of $32 = 0.80 \times 32 = 25.6$
D. 16, 80% of $16 = 0.80 \times 16 = 12.8$
E. 12, 80% of $12 = 0.80 \times 12 = 9.6$

24) Choice D is correct

If the length of the box is 27, then the width of the box is one third of it, 9, and the height of the box is 3 (one third of the width). The volume of the box is:

$$V = lwh = (27)(9)(3) = 729\ cm^3$$

25) Choice B is correct

Plug in 104 for F and then solve for C.

$$C = \frac{5}{9}(F - 32) \Rightarrow C = \frac{5}{9}(104 - 32) \Rightarrow C = \frac{5}{9}(72) = 40$$

SSAT Upper Level Mathematics Practice Test 5 Section 2

1) Choice B is correct

$\frac{17+11}{2} = \frac{28}{2} = 14$ Then, $14 - 11 = 3$

2) Choice C is correct

$\frac{91501}{305} \cong 300.0032 \cong 300$

3) Choice E is correct

Alex's mark = $16 - k$

4) Choice A is correct

The Area that one liter of paint is required: $72cm \times 100cm = 7{,}200cm^2$

Remember: $1\ m^2 = 10{,}000\ cm^2\ (100 \times 100 = 10{,}000), then, 7{,}200cm^2 = 0.72cm^2$

Number of liters of paint we need: $\frac{36}{0.72} = 50$ liters

5) Choice C is correct

Let's review the choices provided:

A. $x = 2 \rightarrow$ The perimeter of the figure is: $2 + 4 + 2 + 2 + 2 = 12 \neq 20$
B. $x = 3 \rightarrow$ The perimeter of the figure is: $2 + 4 + 2 + 3 + 3 = 14 \neq 20$
C. $x = 6 \rightarrow$ The perimeter of the figure is: $2 + 4 + 2 + 6 + 6 = 20 = 20$
D. $x = 9 \rightarrow$ The perimeter of the figure is: $2 + 4 + 2 + 9 + 9 = 26 \neq 20$

E. $x = 12 \rightarrow$ The perimeter of the figure is: $2 + 4 + 2 + 12 + 12 = 32 \neq 20$

6) Choice B is correct

$$750 - 7\frac{7}{15} = 750 - \frac{(7 \times 15) + 7}{15} = 750 - \frac{112}{15} = \frac{(750 \times 15) - 112}{15} = \frac{11{,}138}{15} = 742\frac{8}{15}$$

7) Choice E is correct

Let's review the choices provided:

A. $10 \times \frac{1}{2} = \frac{10}{2} = 5 = 5$

B. $25 \times \frac{1}{5} = \frac{25}{5} = 5 = 5$

C. $2 \times \frac{5}{2} = \frac{10}{2} = 5 = 5$

D. $6 \times \frac{5}{6} = \frac{30}{6} = 5 = 5$

E. $5 \times \frac{1}{5} = \frac{5}{5} = 1 \neq 5$

8) Choice E is correct

Find the difference of each pairs of numbers: $2, 3, 5, 8, 12, 17, 23, \_\_, 38$

The difference of 2 and 3 is 1, 3 and 5 is 2, 5 and 8 is 3, 8 and 12 is 4, 12 and 17 is 5, 17 and 23 is 6, 23 and next number should be 7. The number is $23 + 7 = 30$.

9) Choice E is correct

Number of times that driver rest $= \frac{20}{4} = 5$, Driver's rest time $=$ $1\ hour\ and\ 12\ minutes =$ $72\ minutes$, Then, $5 \times 72\ minutes = 360\ minutes$, $1\ hour = 60\ minutes \rightarrow$ $360\ minutes = 6\ hours$

10) Choice C is correct

Let x be the original price. If the price of the sofa is decreased by 25% to \$420, then: 75% of $x = 420 \Rightarrow 0.75x = 420 \Rightarrow x = 420 \div 0.75 = 560$

11) Choice A is correct

Let the number be A. Then: $x = y\% \times A$. Solve for A. $x = \frac{y}{100} \times A$

Multiply both sides by $\frac{100}{y}$: $x \times \frac{100}{y} = \frac{y}{100} \times \frac{100}{y} \times A \rightarrow A = \frac{100x}{y}$

12) Choice C is correct

Simplify each choice provided.

A. $20 - (4 \times 10) + (6 \times 30) = 20 - 40 + 180 = 160$

B. $\left(\frac{11}{8} \times 72\right) + \left(\frac{125}{5}\right) = 99 + 25 = 124$

C. $\left(\left(\frac{30}{4} + \frac{13}{2}\right) \times 7\right) - \frac{11}{2} + \frac{110}{4} = \left(\left(\frac{30+26}{4}\right) \times 7\right) - \frac{11}{2} + \frac{55}{2} = \left(\left(\frac{56}{4}\right) \times 7\right) + \frac{55-11}{2} =$
$(14 \times 7) + \frac{44}{2} = 98 + 22 = 120$ (this is the answer)

D. $(2 \times 10) + (50 \times 1.5) + 15 = 20 + 75 + 15 = 110$

E. $\frac{481}{6} + \frac{121}{3} = \frac{481+242}{6} = 120.5$

13) Choice E is correct

$3y + 5 < 29 \rightarrow 3y < 29 - 5 \rightarrow 3y < 24 \rightarrow y < 8$

Only choice E is less than 8.

14) Choice D is correct

The capacity of a red box is 20% bigger than the capacity of a blue box and it can hold 30 books. Therefore, we want to find a number that 20% bigger than that number is 30. Let x be that number. Then: $1.20 \times x = 30$, Divide both sides of the equation by 1.2. Then:$x = \frac{30}{1.20} = 25$

15) Choice D is correct

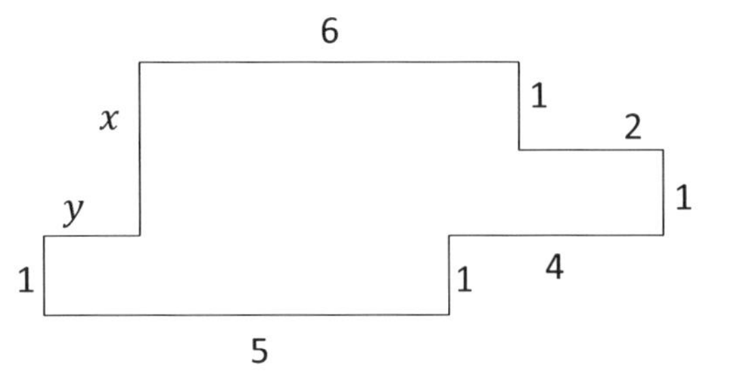

$x + 1 = 1 + 1 + 1 \rightarrow x = 2$

$y + 6 + 2 = 5 + 4 \rightarrow y + 8 = 9 \rightarrow y = 1$

Then, the perimeter is:

$1 + 5 + 1 + 4 + 1 + 2 + 1 + 6 + 2 + 1 = 24$

16) Choice D is correct

Amount of available petrol in tank: $50.2 - 5.82 - 25.9 + 10.31 = 28.79$ liters

17) Choice E is correct

We have two equations and three unknown variables, therefore x cannot be obtained.

18) Choice A is correct

Perimeter of figure A is: $2\pi r = 2\pi \frac{16}{2} = 16\pi = 16 \times 3 = 48$, Area of figure B is: $5 \times 12 = 60$,
$Average = \frac{48+60}{2} = \frac{108}{2} = 54$

19) Choice E is correct

Let put some values for a and b.

If $a = 9$ and $b = 2 \rightarrow a \times b = 18 \rightarrow \frac{18}{3} = 6 \rightarrow$ 18 is divisible by 3 then:

A. $a + b = 9 + 2 = 11$ is not divisible by 3

B. $3a - b = (3 \times 9) - 2 = 27 - 2 = 25$ is not divisible by 3
C. $a - 3b + 1 = 9 - (3 \times 2) + 1 = 7$ is not divisible by 3
D. $\frac{a}{b} = \frac{9}{2}$ is not divisible by 3

E. $4 \times a \times b \rightarrow 4 \times 11 \times 3 = 132$. It is divisible by 3. If you choose any other numbers for a and b you will get the same result.

20) Choice D is correct

The area of ΔBED is 16, then: $\frac{4 \times AB}{2} = 16 \rightarrow 4 \times AB = 32 \rightarrow AB = 8$

The area of ΔBDF is 18, then: $\frac{3 \times BC}{2} = 18 \rightarrow 3 \times BC = 36 \rightarrow BC = 12$

The perimeter of the rectangle is = $2 \times (8 + 12) = 40$

21) Choice B is correct

The area of trapezoid is: $\left(\frac{8+12}{2}\right) \times x = 100 \rightarrow 10x = 100 \rightarrow x = 10$. $y = \sqrt{3^2 + 4^2} = 5$

Perimeter is: $12 + 10 + 8 + 5 = 35$

22) Choice E is correct

Based on triangle similarity theorem: $\frac{a}{a+b} = \frac{c}{3} \rightarrow c = \frac{3a}{a+b} = \frac{3\sqrt{3}}{3\sqrt{3}} = 1 \rightarrow$ area of shaded region is: $\left(\frac{c+3}{2}\right)(b) = \frac{4}{2} \times 2\sqrt{3} = 4\sqrt{3}$

23) Choice C is correct

$$712 \div 3 = \frac{712}{3} = \frac{700 + 10 + 2}{3} = \frac{700}{3} + \frac{10}{3} + \frac{2}{3}$$

24) Choice D is correct

$$\frac{2}{5} \times 25 = \frac{50}{5} = 10$$

25) Choice E is correct

A. $x = \frac{1}{2} \rightarrow \frac{5}{9} + \frac{1}{2} = \frac{10+9}{18} = \frac{19}{18} \cong 1.056 < 2$
B. $x = \frac{3}{5} \rightarrow \frac{5}{9} + \frac{3}{5} = \frac{25+27}{45} = \frac{52}{45} \cong 1.16 < 2$
C. $x = \frac{4}{5} \rightarrow \frac{5}{9} + \frac{4}{5} = \frac{25+36}{45} = \frac{61}{45} \cong 1.36 < 2$
D. $x = \frac{4}{3} \rightarrow \frac{5}{9} + \frac{4}{3} = \frac{5+12}{9} = \frac{17}{9} \cong 1.89 < 2$
E. $x = \frac{5}{3} \rightarrow \frac{5}{9} + \frac{5}{3} = \frac{5+15}{9} = \frac{20}{9} \cong 2.2 > 2$

"Effortless Math Education" Publications

Effortless Math authors' team strives to prepare and publish the best quality Mathematics learning resources to make learning Math easier for all. We hope that our publications help you learn Math in an effective way and prepare for the test.

We all in Effortless Math wish you good luck and successful studies!

Effortless Math Authors

www.EffortlessMath.com

... So Much More Online!

- FREE Math lessons
- More Math learning books!
- Mathematics Worksheets
- Online Math Tutors

Need a PDF version of this book?

Visit www.EffortlessMath.com

Receive the PDF version of this book or get another FREE book!

Thank you for using our Book!

Do you LOVE this book?

Then, you can get the PDF version of this book or another book absolutely FREE!

Please email us at:

info@EffortlessMath.com

for details.

Made in the USA
Las Vegas, NV
15 September 2023